T0062986

CHRONICLES OF A RELUCTANT IMMIGRANT

Also by Raj Pandya

Introduction to WLLs - Application and deployment for Fixed
And Broadband Services (John Wiley & Sons 2004)

Mobile and Personal Communication Services and Systems
(John Wiley & Sons 1999)

CHRONICLES OF A RELUCTANT IMMIGRANT

A Cross Cultural Journey

RAJ PANDYA

PARTRIDGE

A Penguin Random House Company

Copyright © 2015 by Raj Pandya.

ISBN:	Hardcover	978-1-4828-4088-9
	Softcover	978-1-4828-4089-6
	eBook	978-1-4828-4087-2

All rights reserved. No part of this book may be used or reproduced by any means, graphic, electronic, or mechanical, including photocopying, recording, taping or by any information storage retrieval system without the written permission of the publisher except in the case of brief quotations embodied in critical articles and reviews.

Because of the dynamic nature of the Internet, any web addresses or links contained in this book may have changed since publication and may no longer be valid. The views expressed in this work are solely those of the author and do not necessarily reflect the views of the publisher, and the publisher hereby disclaims any responsibility for them.

To order additional copies of this book, contact
Partridge India
000 800 10062 62
orders.india@partridgepublishing.com

www.partridgepublishing.com/india

CONTENTS

INDIA (1972 – 1974)

CANADA (1974 – 1990)

AUSTRALIA (1990 – 1992)

CANADA (1992 – 2012)

Author's Note

I have tried to describe, to the best of my recollections, the events, which took place over a period of eight decades. It is therefore possible that my recollections of these events may some what differ from those of others. Where it was necessary and appropriate to maintain the anonymity and privacy of individuals involved, I have changed (or omitted) their names as well as changed relevant identifying characteristics and details such as their occupations and localities where they resided.

For my wife, without her there would be no story
to tell, and for our children and grandchildren,
without them there would be no reason to tell
the story

Preface

This autobiographical journey is a multi-dimenioned narrative encompassing a number of distinct though interwoven themes. It is a coming of age story of a boy (RAJ) from an obscure small town in India born and raised in an orthodox Hindu family. It is a love story that spans distant continents and different cultures. It is a story of a mixed race and cross cultural marriage played out in the East and the West. It is a commentary about the history and culture of the people and places the protagonist encounters over the journey and the times he lives through. Finally it is the story of a well educated man who is frustrated and disheartened because he is unable to find professional fulfilment in his country of birth, and reluctantly looks to the West for better opportunities, where he finally immigrates and succeeds in salvaging his moribund professional career and earns the recognition he deserves.

The narrative opens when the author arrives in Canada at the age of twenty nine to pursue graduate studies at the University of Toronto. During this visit he falls in love with a Canadian girl (MARGARET) who grew up on a family farm in Ontario. This event turns out to be an inflection point in his life which challenges his past and alters his future in unexpected and unprecedented ways. The rest of the narrative is the story of his journey leading up to this critical event and what follows after it in a cross cultural context.

After their marriage in India they lived for extended periods in the city of Jabalpur in India and, their two children had a full immersion in the Indian culture and way of life. However, when they permanently moved to Canada in 1974, the children were only nine and four years old. In the absence of any meaningful and sustained contact with India or the Indian community in Canada, they grew up within the Canadian culture. Any memories they have of their childhood in India are at best vague and only sporadic. Their spouses are Caucasian and their children, of course, have little idea of their mixed ancestry. The book therefore evolved from the author's desire to leave a written record of his life's journey prior to and after meeting Margaret so that their progeny could trace the source of their genetic pool and the story behind it.

However, when some of our friends who have better literary credentials than the author read the developing narrative, they unanimously felt that it deserves better recognition than simply as the genealogical record for a limited audience. Considering that it is an eventful story with cross cultural dimensions, told in an imaginative and informative manner, the ad hoc consensus was that the narrative would resonate well with a much larger segment of the English speaking population in many countries which led to its final development into a book.

The Moving Finger writes: and, having writ, Moves on: nor all thy Piety nor Wit
shall lure it back to cancel half a Line,
nor all thy Tears wash out a Word of it.
Omar Khayyam (1048 – 1131)
Philosopher, Poet, Mathematician, Astronomer

PROLOGUE

It is late afternoon on a summer day in one of the many little towns in Central India. The entire household of a middle class Gujarati Brahmin family is gathered on the front veranda of their large ancestral home. There is no Western style furniture in the room, only a couple of *dhurries* (cotton rugs) spread out on the floor and a *jhula* (swing), the latter being a common item in households belonging to their community. It is the day when the family priest and astrologer will bring over and read the horoscope which he has prepared for the latest addition to the family – a nine-month-old baby boy. The baby, however, is happily enjoying an afternoon nap on his mother's lap and is completely oblivious to the occasion and its importance. The grandmother is entertaining the rest of his siblings by telling stories from such Hindu epics as: *Mahabharat* and *Ramayan*. The father, the family patriarch, is working on his accounts and becoming increasingly impatient with the tardiness of the priest.

Finally, the priest arrives and removes the boy's horoscope from his cloth bag and spreads out the long narrow scroll on the *dhurrie* in front of him. The top of the horoscope shows the zodiac chart with the position of the sun and various planets on the exact date, time, and the geographic coordinates of the boy's birth. The rest of the text on the scroll is written in Sanskrit, the ancient language in which most Hindu scriptures are written, and the priest proceeds to translate the highlights from the Sanskrit text. The text elaborates on how the relative positions of the various planets will influence the child's personality and affect his life hereafter. In the last category, the priest informs the family that, as an adult, the boy is likely to travel far and wide, experience many cultures, and may not always operate within the strict bounds of past traditions.

The parents digest the information provided by the priest with a mixture of pride and trepidation, and ask the priest a few more questions such as: will there be periods in the boy's life where he might be in danger of developing serious illness or worse, and if so what kind of *poojas*, (religious rituals) the priest would recommend to protect him from such dangers. Soon the reading is finished and the priest hands over the horoscope to the family patriarch for safe keeping. He in turn locks it in a cupboard alongside the horoscopes of his other children. The horoscope would rarely be revisited until the boy reaches marriageable age and the search for a suitable bride is undertaken. According to the family tradition, a marriage proposal would not proceed any further unless the horoscopes of the prospective bride and groom are fully compatible. In a culture of arranged marriages where the prospective marriage partners have little direct contact prior to the wedding, this matching of horoscopes is meant to ensure that the personalities and preferences of the husband and wife will be compatible, and hopefully lead to love, trust and harmony in their married life.

CANADA (1961 – 1964)

****

CHAPTER 1

Adapting to the Western culture and customs

First twenty four hours

A few weeks after my 29th birthday, on a night in early September, 1961, I landed at the small airport in Ottawa en route to Toronto, Canada. After the long and tiring flight, I was dragging my butt as well as a huge, mostly empty, suitcase. I was hoping to fill the suitcase with all the nifty gadgets and goodies available in North America so that I could, impress my family and friends on my return home to India, where such luxuries were scarce. At 5 feet 9 inches in height and weighing only 110 pounds, a very skinny guy dragging a huge suitcase must have been an amusing sight to behold. After spending almost 30 hours with many stops on my first trip from India to Canada I was very tired and disoriented. On the other hand, I had spent almost 30 years with many stops along the way on my journey from an obscure little town in India to the threshold of the West. This was an opportunity I had been looking forward to for a long time and I was very excited at the prospect of spending the next two years in Canada as a graduate student at the University of Toronto.

In those days, there were no non-stop flights from New Delhi to London. The British Overseas Airways Corporation (now British Airways) turbo jet aircraft had stopped in Teheran, Ankara, and Frankfurt before finally arriving, a few hours behind schedule, at London's Heathrow Airport. As a consequence, I missed my connecting BOAC flight to Montreal and was transferred to a Trans Canada Airways (now Air Canada) flight that did not reach Montreal until late in the evening, resulting in an even later arrival in Ottawa. Fortunately, the TCA flight from London to Montreal was three-quarters empty, so I was able to stretch out and grab a couple of hours of sleep. On that flight, I also had my first experience of drinking wine and eating a steak dinner. The latter, of course, broke the Hindu dietary restriction against eating beef. However, I was unable to keep it all down and, to my embarrassment; I had to make use of the barf bag.

My graduate studies at the University of Toronto were being funded by the Canadian Government under a Commonwealth program and my travel itinerary was arranged by the Canadian High Commission in New Delhi. At the Ottawa airport, I was met and greeted by a Canadian Government official who drove me, along with a couple of other students from India under the same program, to the Ottawa YMCA on Metcalfe Street for an overnight stay. He gave me a cash advance and directions to his office on Wellington Street where I was to meet him the next morning for further briefing. I was glad to receive the cash advance because with the strict foreign exchange restrictions in India, I had left India with only ten dollars in my pocket. As soon as we said good night, I was more than ready to fall into a long, uninterrupted sleep.

My introduction to the Western way of life began the next morning when I entered the common facilities for my morning shower. The sight of several stark naked men walking around in the room tested my strong sense of modesty. I had never come across such a sight before, even when I was living in university residences back home. In India it is customary for men to keep their under shorts on while taking a shower in a common facility. However, I quickly overcame my unease and opted to "do as the Romans do." After living in Canada for a while, I became quite comfortable stripping down in locker rooms to share the showers and the sauna or hot tub in the buff. After the shower, I got ready for my day in Ottawa, and walked out into the fresh, sunny autumn morning in search of breakfast, before my appointment with the Canadian Government contact. I enjoyed my first Canadian breakfast of orange juice, fried eggs (sunny side up), bacon, toast and coffee. After breakfast I walked up to Wellington Street, admiring the majesty and the architectural style of the Canadian Parliament buildings, which rose before me.

I spent most of the morning with my Canadian Government contact who gave me extensive advice on how to survive a Canadian winter, including such essentials as the layering principle, the need for a good pair of winter boots, a warm overcoat, and a toque. He also advised me to open a bank account as soon I was settled in Toronto so that he could arrange to deposit my financial support directly in my account. This consisted of a living allowance of $165 per month and a $300 lump sum for books and clothing. He provided me with the travel documents for the overnight train to Toronto leaving that night, and directions to the Ottawa railway station, which was then located across from the Chateau Laurier Hotel. He also advised me to get in touch with Mrs. Kay Riddell, who was arranging for my temporary accommodation in Toronto. She was the Director of an organisation called Friendly Relations with Overseas Students (FROS) set up by the University of Toronto to provide a soft landing for overseas students into the new country, and to help them become familiar with the Canadian culture and way of life. FROS later developed into a much bigger entity - the International House of the University of Toronto.

After our meeting finished in the late morning, I took a leisurely stroll on the grounds of the Parliament buildings, enjoying the spectacular views of the Ottawa River and the lush foliage on the opposite bank. I also phoned Dr. Shrivastava, a professional colleague from India, who was working in Ottawa. He invited me to his home for a visit and dinner that evening before I caught the train to Toronto. My colleague's apartment was located in a three-level triplex near the Ottawa River. Not knowing on which level he lived, I walked up to the first door I saw and rang the bell. When the door opened, I experienced the second unexpected sight of the day. Standing in front of me was an attractive young lady wearing only a two-piece bathing suit. Apart from Hollywood movies, I had never seen a female in a bathing suit – let alone such a skimpy bikini – and I never expected to see one at any place other than a swimming pool or a beach. The scene was so alien to me that I was temporarily tongue-tied. Before I managed to apologize for knocking on the wrong door, she guessed that I was looking for Dr. Shrivastava and directed me to the basement flat. In the course of the evening, when I mentioned my encounter with the lady upstairs to Mrs. Shrivastava, she had a good chuckle and told me that the woman was, in fact, a very friendly and helpful neighbour who often sun-bathed on her back patio in the afternoon.

After a nice Indian dinner (it would be a long time before my next Indian meal), the jetlag finally caught up with me and I fell sound asleep on the living room chair. By the time I woke up, it was time to call a taxi and go to the Ottawa station for my overnight train journey to Toronto. As the train became ready for boarding, the conductor directed me to my reserved sleeping accommodation. He made the bed, helped me climb up to the upper birth and pulled the curtains, leaving me in a coffin-like space. Before leaving, he informed me that he would wake me up half an hour before we arrived in Toronto. The whole process was extremely smooth and painless compared to my experiences on Indian trains and train stations.

I turned off the light and waited for sleep, which was a long time coming, due to a combination of excitement about my upcoming time in Toronto and the residual jet lag. I started to review my impressions and experiences from my first twenty-four hours in Canada. This was my first experience operating entirely within a Western culture. My knowledge and understanding of the Western culture was based on the English language books which I had read, and the Hollywood films that I had seen over the past dozen or more years. I concluded that the day had unfolded mostly as I had expected, and that my second-hand knowledge should serve me well as a foundation for further understanding this new cultural environment and comfortably navigating through it in my daily life. The two incidents that I had not anticipated and was not adequately prepared for were the shower scene at the YMCA and the encounter with the young lady in the bikini. My instinctive sense of modesty or prudishness resulted from the prevailing attitudes in India at the time, which, to a large extent, continues today. Notwithstanding the popular Bollywood movies with their sexy costumes, raunchy dance and song routines and sexual overtones, the average Indian man or woman is culturally conditioned to be prudish in matters concerning nudity and sex.

Getting settled in 'Toronto the Good'

It was close to dawn, although still dark outside, when the train conductor delivered the wake up knock. I managed to change from my pyjamas into regular clothes in the confined space of the sleeping berth. When I looked out the window, I could see the shimmering lights of the city in the distance. The train finally arrived at Toronto's Union Station and I stepped down on the platform. The platform was ill-lit and very quiet, devoid of any life other than the few alighting passengers. I proceeded to the baggage counters in the main concourse and collected my big suitcase. It was only 6:30 in the morning and too early to call Mrs. Riddell to get instructions about my next move. I sat down on a bench and looked around the impressive concourse with its vaulted ceiling and huge windows. Once the travellers from the overnight train from Ottawa had departed, the place was completely empty apart from a few people in railway uniforms. Once again my thoughts wandered back to the scenes at railway stations in India that I had observed and been part of over the years.

Railway stations in India are living organisms which display all aspects of everyday life, such as cooking, eating, drinking, bathing, sleeping – even producing and raising children can be observed in any large railway station in India. When a train arrives at the platform, the activity level rises to a fever pitch with families hurrying behind red-shirted porters balancing large loads of baggage on their heads, hawkers selling hot and cold drinks, hot snacks, paperback books and magazines, and local souvenirs from their push carts, and train passengers running back and forth filling pitchers of drinking water or buying food for their journey. For the five or ten minutes between the arrival and departure of a train, it feels like a pandemonium has broken out. Once the train departs, life in the station returns to its normal leisurely pace with station dwellers, waiting passengers, and station employees resuming their normal everyday activities. I recall spending many a night sleeping *al fresco* on Indian railway platforms during my travels and becoming part of the landscape of an Indian railway station.

During my high school years, I had lived in Raipur, a mid-sized city in Central India, where train routes to half a dozen destinations intersected. As a teenager, I found the activity at the railway station fascinating and highly entertaining. My favourite pastime on a Sunday afternoon was to walk the few miles to the station to watch the trains from various destinations arrive and depart over the hours. I also enjoyed these trips because they always included a visit to the A.H. Wheeler bookstall at the station. It was the only place in town that carried cheap paperback novels and magazines, and where I was able to briefly browse through them.

It was on these weekly excursions that I initially heard the words Canada and Canadian. After India became independent in 1947, the Indian Railways acquired a number of steam locomotives from Canada which had been made redundant there and replaced by diesel powered locomotives. The Canadian steam engines were put into service in India on long distance express routes. The Canadian steam engines were more powerful and much larger than any we had seen, and they had a very distinctive whistle. As soon as we saw or heard one of these locomotives, we could immediately recognize it as a Canadian model. Since then, the Indian Railways have made considerable progress and the steam locomotives, including the Canadian ones, have been replaced by diesel or electric locomotives.

Dawn finally broke, and early daylight started to filter through the windows of the Union Station. It was getting to be 7:30 in the morning, and I felt it was not too early to call Mrs. Riddell. She was very gracious and welcomed me to Canada and to the University of Toronto. She expressed regret that due to the short notice of my itinerary, she had not been able to arrange for a volunteer to meet me at the train station. She directed me to the YMCA on College Street and gave me directions to the FROS office on Willcocks Street near Spadina Avenue where I was to meet her later in the morning. As the taxi drove me to the YMCA along the expanse of University Avenue, I caught my first glimpse of the city and started to think about the path my journey had taken to finally arrive in Toronto and the incidents in my life that had influenced this path. Although my interest in Canada had been piqued when I was a teenager watching the Canadian locomotives, I had no inkling at the time that I would ever have a chance to travel abroad after completing my professional education. In fact, my desire to see the city of Toronto and to study at the University of Toronto had been inspired by a few chance encounters.

The first incident, probably of primary significance, involved a meeting on a train with a young Canadian globetrotter. I was returning from a job interview in Bombay (Mumbai) to Agra, site of the Taj Mahal' where I was an intern at an Army establishment. I was travelling in one of the economy class carriages which are always packed to over capacity. I was congratulating myself for having grabbed a seat in the melee that ensued when the train pulled up at the platform. Just before the train was ready to depart, I noticed a young Caucasian man come into the carriage, wearing shorts, a tee shirt and sandals, and carrying a rucksack. Most of the passengers in the carriage were staring at him with some curiosity because, in those days, it was rare to see a white person travelling economy class in India. This was still a number of years before Western hippies began to make their way into India in search of *gurus* and *ganja,* and such a sight became more common. I made some room for him to sit down, and he was very polite, thanked me and introduced himself as Thomas Williams from Toronto, Canada. We started talking and he told me that he had recently finished his studies and was travelling around the world, earning money as he went, with temporary odd jobs. He had just arrived from South Africa on a cargo ship, working as a deck hand and was now on his way to Agra to see the famous Taj Mahal. He had no idea where he was going to stay in Agra, so I offered to share with him my living accommodation which was a one-room studio over an Indian sweet seller's shop

He readily accepted my offer. In Agra, we rented a couple of bikes and spent the next couple of days exploring the city's examples of *Mugal* architecture, including the Taj Mahal, the Red Fort, and Emperor Akbar's tomb.

While Thomas stayed with me, we had many conversations during which he told me that he had left behind a girlfriend in Toronto, whom he had dated since high school and they would probably get married after he returned to Toronto and got a permanent job. I was very impressed by his adventurous spirit and appreciated the fact that, unlike India and most of the East, young people in Canada and the West are raised by their parents to be independent and are free to make their life choices from an early age. After two days, Thomas left for the rest of his travels in India at the end of which he intended to find another cargo ship to take him to South East Asia and Japan, on to Australia, and finally back home to Canada. Unfortunately, I did not bother to ask him for his address in Toronto, never imagining that I would ever be there myself, and my subsequent efforts to locate him after I arrived in Toronto were fruitless.

After checking in at the YMCA, I started getting ready for the day ahead with some sense of anticipation and excitement. The YMCA desk attendant recommended a nearby restaurant called Fran's as a very good place for breakfast. The recommendation was well founded and I returned to the restaurant frequently during my stay in Toronto and even in later years when I was visiting Toronto on short trips with my family – especially because I was hooked on their sinful banana splits. After finishing my hearty breakfast, I started out along College Street towards Spadina Avenue to meet Mrs. Riddell. On my way there, I began to observe the sights and sounds of this major Canadian metropolis. I passed such Toronto landmarks as the Eaton College Street store, the Toronto General Hospital, the Ontario Legislature, the Ontario Hydro building, and various U of T buildings along College Street. I soon noticed that apart from the streetcar noise, there was little noise from car horns. This made an immediate impression on me because in city centres in India the noise level from the constant honking of car, bus, and truck horns is deafening as these vehicles compete with each other, as well as with other vehicles and pedestrians (and sometimes stray cows and dogs) for a portion of the narrow roads. I also considered the history of Toronto which I had read about in the small information booklet provided by the Canadian High Commission in India, and how closely it resembled the history of the India's two largest cities – Bombay and Calcutta. All three were incorporated by the British colonizers around the same period (the first half of the 19ᵗʰ century), from relatively small settlements on marshy flats which were less than hospitable to human life and were prone to frequent outbreaks of such terrible diseases as typhus, cholera and malaria. All three settlements developed into mega cities and became important centres for commerce, finance and culture.

As I reached Spadina Avenue, I turned north, passing the Banting and Best Labs and Borden's Milk Depot. Finally, I arrived at the FROS office which turned out to be a two-storey house, originally a family residence. Mrs. Riddell was a pleasant lady in her early fifties. She introduced me to the two secretaries in the FROS office and took me for a tour of the building. The front room was used as a common room for students to drop in during lunch hour. The upstairs rooms were used as study rooms and for storage. Mrs. Riddell gave me some general information about the role of FROS and about the University and invited me to drop in anytime to see her or use the facilities. She also told me that the University currently did not have graduate student residences, but rooms were available for rent in various neighbourhoods around the University. She advised me to get a list of such accommodations from the Housing Office and to visit the available rooms to find suitable accommodation. One of the students lounging in the front room kindly offered to walk me to the new Engineering Building on St. George Street so that I could report to the Head of the Electrical Engineering Department to sort out the details of my graduate studies program.

I met with my graduate studies supervisor, Professor Ham, and decided on my course list for the next two terms. The next stop was the Student Housing Office where I ran into an Egyptian student pursuing the same course as I and who was also looking for a room to rent. Fortunately, he was with a friend who had a car which made it easier to check out the various possibilities. We selected about half-a-dozen possibilities and drove around to inspect them. Finally, we decided on a place on a street not far from the university campus which had two rooms available on the second floor, with a small kitchen and an unheated solarium. My room was about 12 by 10 feet, with a small clothes cupboard, a single bed, a small dresser, and a student desk and chair. It looked out on the back yard which had a mature cherry tree. The location was very convenient being a short walking distance to the University, the Toronto Public Library and a streetcar stop on College Street. I was able to move into my new accommodations the next day and I stayed there until I left Toronto to return home to India.

Our landlord, Mr. Asahi was a Canadian of Japanese descent and his wife was a Caucasian. They had a daughter in her teens and a younger son. There was another tenant in the house – a young British lady in her mid to late-twenties who shared a room with the landlord's daughter. Mr. Asahi the landlord was a rather quiet and taciturn person while Mrs Asahi the landlady was very outgoing and worked at a Department Store. We mostly dealt with her for our day-to-day needs as tenants. Although the landlord and his wife were average in terms of their looks, their daughter and son had inherited an optimal combination of Oriental and Caucasian features and were both quite attractive.

On our landlady's recommendation, we visited the Kensington Market and Honest Ed's to stock the kitchen with basic provisions and get supplies for our daily personal use. I enjoyed walking around the Kensington Market because its small shops with wares spilling out on to the sidewalk and the predominance of pedestrians over cars reminded me of Indian bazaars. However, an Indian bazaar is a much more chaotic, colourful, noisy and vibrant place which immediately assaults your visual, olfactory, and auditory senses. The Indian bazaar is not only full of people shopping for a wide variety of goods ranging from fruits and vegetables to clothing and jewellery, it is also usually populated with cows and goats trying to grab edibles from the open stalls, as well as stray dogs and cats. Compared to the Kensington Market, the Honest Ed's experience was more muted, although it carried a broad variety of items, from wedding dresses to cheap kitchen wares, in a carnival-like atmosphere.

Cultural Adjustments

Soon after my arrival, I noticed that in Canada it is common practice to call everyone by their first name, except when children address their parents (Mom and Dad) and grandparents (Grandma and Grandpa), or sometimes add 'uncle' or 'aunt' if they are addressing their elder relatives or family friends. In most major Indian languages, there is a very specific term or mode of address for every family relationship which extends well beyond parents and grandparents. First names (sometimes abbreviated) are only used to address children or teens, domestic servants and low-level office employees, like *peons* (gofers). I was certain that my full first name "Rajendra" was a non-starter for Canadian tongues and needed a suitable abbreviation that was short and simple. I considered a number of options and finally I decided on 'Raj' because it was the shortest with little room for further abbreviation. However, my landlady persisted in calling me 'Roger' until the day I left. The widespread use of first names to address each other perhaps reflects the fact that in spite of being a former Britain colony, Canada did not develop as a feudal society and its culture is essentially egalitarian, with very little evidence of class or caste structures which are so pervasive in India. In the context of using first names, I recall becoming a member of the local Rotary Club a few years after returning to India. I found that the Rotary Club had a policy (imported from the West) that members should address each other by their first names. However, in the absence of proper social and cultural underpinnings in the Indian society, I found the practice rather contrived and phony.

Besides the unfamiliar cold climate, the other biggest adjustment for me was the unfamiliar food, with its high non-vegetarian content. A majority of Indians are vegetarians, and in my case the problem was further compounded by the fact that I was born and brought up in a Brahmin family which was vegetarian, with very strict rules on who can cook the food, how it is cooked, and how it is served and eaten. For example, when I was growing up, women in our household were not allowed to cook during their menstrual period. The lady, always a member of the family, who was to prepare the meals, had to first have a bath and change into a special sari, reserved for cooking and handling food. There was no question of having meat or poultry in our house and little opportunity of encountering them outside. I had few occasions to eat meat, fish, or poultry until I was in my twenties – and only very sporadically. As well, the food I encountered in Canada was much blander than Indian cuisine which is characterized by liberal use of a variety of spices. However, considering factors like my woefully limited culinary repertoire, non availability of ingredients for Indian meals, and busy schedule at the university, I opted to have a quick breakfast of toast and tea at home and mostly depended on neighbourhood restaurants and the Hart House cafeteria for my lunch and dinner.

When I got a craving for spicy food, I went to a Greek restaurant on Yonge Street and had a plate of spaghetti and meat sauce laced liberally with hot red pepper flakes. When summer arrived, I discovered a small pizzeria on Yonge Street near Bloor Street and visited it frequently to have a piping hot pizza, hoping that my palate would be fooled into believing that it was a *Tandoori Roti* or *Naan* covered with roasted vegetables and meat. There were few restaurants in downtown Toronto in the early sixties that served ethnic food, except for the row of Chinese restaurants on Dundas Street which served mostly Cantonese dishes. Unfortunately, the hot and spicy Szechuan cuisine had not yet hit the Toronto Chinese restaurant scene. Whatever good or bad effects it had on my long-term health, the Canadian diet led to a very visible outcome – it put some much needed flesh on my bones. After 28 months in Toronto, I had gained almost 30 pounds and weighed close to 140 pounds by the time I left for India.

As a visitor from India, I was frequently asked – and am still asked – why Hindus consider cows sacred and are averse to killing them or eating their flesh. The most plausible explanation I have come across is advanced by Nirad C. Chaudhuri in his book Continent of Circe. According to Chaudhuri, when the Aryans first came to India from Central Asia around 1500 BCE, they brought with them a large herd of humped-back cattle, a superior species not indigenous to the Indian sub-continent. The original immigrant Aryans not only killed these cattle for food, but also used them as sacrifices in their religious rituals. However, after a few centuries, the population of humped back cattle had drastically depleted and in an attempt to save the species, the priestly class declared these animals to be sacred and decreed that slaughtering of cows and eating beef would be strictly prohibited and considered an unforgivable sin for a Hindu.

The ever polite Canadian

Another aspect of my new environment that I had to quickly adapt to was the Canadian version of polite behaviour. I soon noticed that Canadians tend to say "please" and "thank you" all the time and not doing so is considered rude. I found this rather unusual and over the top, at least until I got used to the ritual. Nobel Prize winning economist, Amritya Sen mentions in his book: Identity and Violence, that one of his professors at Cambridge University told him, "The Japanese are too polite; you Indians are too rude; and the Chinese are just right." I personally believe that Canadians are way up there near the Japanese on the politeness scale, and unfortunately I have to agree with the Cambridge professor's observation that Indians are generally an impolite bunch. Anyone who has spent even a short time in India and has had the misfortune to deal with any government bureaucrat or an employee of a publicly-owned organization like Indian Railways or Air India can attest to this pervasive attitude which continues to persist because there is little incentive for politeness or punishment for rudeness when dealing with Joe Public.

The custom of saying "please" and "thank you" is viewed quite differently in the context of daily life in India. The prevailing attitude in Indian households is that one does not need to say "please" or "thank you" when one asks a domestic servant for a cup of tea and he/she brings it to you. In this context, one is not asking for a favour – a favour allows room for refusal – nor is the servant bestowing a favour. The task is a part of his/her job description and is viewed as a straight exchange of service for payment. In a close family environment, the situation is somewhat different: there generally exists a strong (though implicit) sense of entitlement/obligation in day-to-day transactions between members of the family and the exchange of so-called 'favours' is considered as routine give-and-take within the family. In India, if I was to formally thank a close family member for something he/she did for me, he/she would feel insulted, thinking that I was treating them as an outsider and not as a member of my close family. Even though I have now fully adapted to Canadian standards of politeness, I still feel a bit strange whenever I thank my daughter when she hands me a glass of water.

Although the sense of closeness and entitlement within the extended family in India provides a certain sense of security, there is also a downside. This sense of entitlement can have a very negative effect in a broader social sense, unless one applies some judgment in navigating the moral and ethical issues that often arise. For example, when I was a professor at an engineering school in India, it was not uncommon for a distant cousin and his/her mother to drop in and invoking our distant family relationship, to request, or almost demand that I use my influence (which was not very much) to improve the chances of the cousin being admitted to the engineering school. When this sense of entitlement expands on a wider scale, for example to the members of a caste, community or tribe, the rules of fairness cease to apply, leading to widespread nepotism and corruption – as is now the case in India and many other developing countries around the world.

Returning to Canadian customs of polite behaviour, it was not long before I started to say 'please' and 'thank you' whenever I could remember to do so (which was not always the case). Like my daughter, who keeps reminding her six-year-old son to say 'please' and 'thank you', my landlady diligently reminded me every time I forgot to use these terms in her presence. Between my landlady and Mrs. Riddell, whom I saw frequently at FROS, I quickly picked up additional tips for navigating in the new environment, such as: not to interrupt another person while he or she is speaking; not to visit a person unannounced or without prior arrangement; not to reach across the person next to you at the dining table for the salt and pepper shaker; not to wander around dressed in pyjamas outside the bedroom, and never to bring an extra person (e.g., a female friend) to a Canadian wedding unless the invitation explicitly contains the words 'and escort' or 'and companion'.

CHAPTER 2

Arrival of spring and a moral dilemma

The fall term at the University was to begin in a few days, and my classes were to be held in diverse locations, including the basement of Sydney Smith Hall, the attic room in the University College, a modern lecture theatre in the new Galbraith Engineering building and an old, dingy classroom in the Skulehouse (the original Engineering Building), the latter so designated by U of T Engineering students in order to project an (false) image as a culturally-challenged group. As a graduate student, I was assigned a workstation and was glad to have a base where I could hang out between classes and do further reading. I also had the privilege of using the Faculty Lounge, where I could have morning and afternoon coffee (five cents per cup) and browse through the latest technical journals. When I learned that the Engineering Students Association had their office and store in the Skulehouse and sold stationery and other items popular with engineering students, I decided to pay a visit and pick up some supplies. When I walked in the door, I saw what looked like a naked lady with flowing blond hair riding a horse. It was actually a life-sized replica of Lady Godiva, the U of T Engineers mascot which was being prepared for the up-coming Frosh Week parade – the Engineering students' Lady Godiva Band, led by Lady Godiva on the horse, was considered the highlight of the annual parade.

Social and cultural life

Soon after arriving in Canada, I had decided that in addition to my academic pursuits, I would participate in and endeavour to learn as much as I could about Canadian social life. I thought that participating in the formal and informal activities sponsored by FROS would serve as the best route towards achieving this goal. One of the objectives of FROS was to encourage overseas students to get together socially with Canadian students as well as with Canadian population at large and frequently arranged events to accomplish such interactions. As a result, during my time in Toronto I was able to engage in a variety of activities which provided me insights into the social and cultural life in Canada, As part of the FROS sponsored activities I attended a Christmas carol singing evening at a Rosedale mansion, a wine and cheese party at the residence of the President of the University, and a number of dinners hosted by people in the community. Among the new experiences I had, included a dinner served on TV tables in front of the television set because the hosts did not want to miss their favourite TV program, and in another instance a couple, rather than cooking at home, decided to take me to their club for dinner. In addition to these social functions, FROS also arranged events to introduce us to some of the typical Canadian recreational activities, such as skating lessons, five-pin bowling nights, curling sessions, and trips to Collingwood for downhill ski lessons. Unfortunately, I could not continue my lessons in skating and downhill skiing (which I regret) due to lack of funds, time, and motivation. However, before leaving Toronto, I did learn to roller skate at a rink on Jarvis Street, and later in my life became sufficiently proficient in cross-country skiing to go out on the trails and enjoy the solitude and beauty of the Canadian woods in winter.

Although I greeted the first snowfall with awe and excitement, and even walked around Queens Park to fully appreciate the experience, by the time February rolled around, I was getting anxious for the warmth of the long-awaited spring. By the end of the winter term in April, I had completed my course requirements and was starting to think about the thesis that would occupy my time for the next year or so. However, the pressure of course work, assignments and end of term examinations was now off so that I felt more relaxed and ready to further explore the local social and cultural practices and institutions. I took advantage of the warmer weather to take part in a number of trips around the Toronto area – some under the auspices of FROS and others with friends I had made during the past few months. I made the obligatory sightseeing trip to Niagara Falls and was duly impressed by the awesome sight of this huge volume of water cascading down the fall. I also had my first experience of watching a Shakespearian play at Stratford, Ontario. My only exposure to Shakespeare had been a difficult slog through *The Merchant of Venice* as part of my undergraduate English literature curriculum. I have to admit that I probably missed half the dialogue at the Stratford performance, although I very much enjoyed the costumes, choreography, and the layout of the Stratford theatre and the pleasant grounds around it, along the appropriately named Avon River. I spent a weekend at the Caledon Farms with a mixed group of students – both overseas students and Canadians. The Farm is owned by the University and is available to any of its associated groups for a retreat. It had separate male and female dormitories, a communal living, dining and kitchen area, and a detached structure generally used for social events. What I remember most about the weekend was the novel experience of sitting and sweating in the sauna (built by some previous U of T students from Scandinavia) and then jumping into the cold waters of an adjacent quarry. I also enjoyed the evening's camp atmosphere – sitting around an open wood fire, eating roasted marshmallows and telling ghost stories. The sight and smell of the campfire made me think of my childhood home - my mother cooking a meal on a simple wood-burning stove in the large open courtyard at our ancestral home. That summer, I also took in many local attractions, including the Canadian National Exhibition, and Black Creek Pioneer Village which represented life in Canada during the nineteenth century. I also toured Maple Leaf Gardens, the home of the Toronto Maple Leafs hockey team, the Toronto Islands and Casa Loma, a European-style castle sitting incongruously in the middle of a modern metropolis. I would have travelled more extensively in this huge country, especially to the Rockies, if time and financial constraints had not limited my options.

By the summer and fall of 1962, I was well into the research for my dissertation, and was spending long hours designing the system that would confirm some theoretical concepts. By this time, I had also made some friends, male and female, and was spending time with them in recreational and social activities. Two of these friends, Bob and Elaine, were senior undergraduate students at Victoria College. The couple were 'going steady' and were headed to the altar once Bob finished his teacher's certificate and found a suitable teaching position. Bob and Elaine, along with a few of their classmates, and I, formed a small group that hung around together. We went on day trips to Caledon Farms, Niagara Falls, or Toronto Centre Island, and frequently spent time in coffee houses in Yorkville, listening to the folk music which was becoming very popular at the time. Occasionally, when we could afford it, we would go down to the basement lounge in the Westbury Hotel which had recently opened on Yonge street, near College street, and have a drink or two and listen to live music.

In early 1963, Bob finished his studies at the University Teachers College. He and Elaine were married at the First Unitarian Congregation at the corner of Avenue Road and St. Clair Avenue, followed by a reception in the beautiful gardens of Casa Loma. Bob was offered a position at an Ottawa high school and they planned to move there at the end of summer. Bob was responsible for initiating me into the world of Canadian politics and politicians. He was a staunch supporter of the New Democratic Party (NDP), a left-of-centre party with socialist leanings and was passionate about the social and political issues of the day. The spring of 1963 was pre-election time in Canada, and the three main political parties, the Progressive Conservatives, the Liberals, and the NDP, were in the thick of electioneering in Toronto. Bob, Elaine and I went down to the Maple Leaf Gardens to listen to their respective leaders. The Liberals won sufficient seats to form the next government with Mike Pearson as the Prime Minister of Canada in April 1963. His administration was instrumental in replacing the existing national flag, the old British Ensign, with the much more distinctively Canadian flag, with the prominent red maple leaf on a white background. He was also instrumental in expanding universal health care to all Canadians.

I completed the requirements for the Master of Applied Science degree from U of T in the spring of 1963 and, instead of going back to India immediately, I had arranged to extend my time in Toronto to acquire some experience in a Canadian work environment. I was assigned to intern at a company located in Scarborough, a distant eastern suburb of Toronto. Fortunately, one of the officers of the company lived in an apartment building on Church Street behind Maple Leaf Gardens, not too far from my rented room, and he kindly offered me a ride to and from the office. My status in the company hierarchy was rather ambiguous. On the one hand, I was treated as part of the management because I was not on an hourly wage and was not part of the day-to-day manufacturing operations. On the other hand, I also worked with the guys on the shop floor – I had to build my experimental system in the shop with the help of various technicians. So I made friends on both sides of the management divide and was always invited to management picnics and Christmas lunches, as well as to parties thrown by people in the shop, including the big party thrown by one of the shop guys who won the Irish Sweepstakes.

Significant events – personal and otherwise

On a personal level, while I was in the middle of my research for my thesis, I received the sad news that after a long illness, my mother had passed away – she was only 62 years old. I was saddened and upset, mainly because I had not been able to spend any extended time with her after leaving home at an early age to pursue my studies. She did visit me from time to time for short periods when I was employed as a teacher at the Engineering College. However, as a bachelor, I was unable to provide the type of family atmosphere in which she would have felt more comfortable and less lonely.

My mother was a kind, compassionate and generous lady, but she had not had an easy life. She was born into a well-to-do family in the state of Andhra Pradesh, which was part of Madras Province before India gained independence. Her father was a middleman who sold upscale jewellery and well-designed ornaments to the rich Rajas and Maharajas during the British Raj. In accordance with the traditions of the time, her marriage was arranged by her parents; and she was married at the age of 12 (my father was 14) into a family that lived in central India, more than four hundred miles away. She started her married life when she was in her mid-teens in a place where the language and culture were very different. The only consolation was that both families belonged to the same community and spoke a common language (Gujarati). One can only imagine the isolation and loneliness she must have felt as a girl barely out of her childhood. She would have found the local language, the food, the customs and the culture completely alien to her, and she would have had little rapport with the people around her in her new home. To her credit, she faced these odds with fortitude and good humour and raised seven children while running the household of an orthodox Brahmin family. In addition, she learned to speak, read and write Hindi, the regional language, and became an avid reader who read to us whenever time and circumstances permitted. I was a long way away from my home and family and there was no one close to me with whom I could share my grief for the loss of this gentle, loving and nurturing soul.

During the period of my stay in Canada a number of very significant, and sometimes scary, events took place on the world stage. The most unnerving of these was the Cuban missile crisis which brought the world to the brink of nuclear confrontation. Other significant developments on the international front included: the assassination of the South Vietnamese President and the escalation of the Vietnamese War, the incursion by Chinese troops into India and the resulting Sino-Indian conflict; the establishment of segregated black townships (Bantu lands) and the tightening of the apartheid regime in South Africa. It was also the period when the first American man was safely launched into space and President Kennedy promised that America would put a man on the moon within the decade. The desegregation of schools in the Southern States gave an impetus to the civil rights movement in America, and finally, the most tragic event of all was the untimely death of President Kennedy at the hands of a lone assassin.

Life with the Asahis

My home life away from the University was coming along nicely, and I got along quite well with my landlady and the other occupants of the house. Initially, since everyone was working or going to school, I would have the house to myself if I returned from the University early in the afternoon. Later, my landlady lost her job because of some irregularity in her job performance. Since she did not have a job any more, she passed her time reading paperback novels, which were marketed as romantic and sexy fiction in those days and were prominently displayed in every drugstore. She was now generally at home and often insisted that I join her for tea and a chat whenever I appeared to be available. She often talked about her childhood in a small town and about the pros and cons of living in a large city like Toronto.

For some reason though, the topic of her courtship with Mr Asahi which led to their marriage never surfaced during these occasional tête-à-têtes. Judging from their daughter's age, they were probably married soon after the end of the war in the Pacific. In the early period of my time in Canada, I was not aware of the treatment of Canadian citizens of Japanese ancestry during World War II and I did not give much thought to the unusual nature of their mixed-race marriage, especially to the potential difficulties they would have encountered. However, some time later I read the novel Obasan by the Canadian author Joy Kogawa about a family's heart ranching experiences when Japanese-Canadians were striped of all their rights, deprived of all their worldly assets and placed in isolated internment camps for the duration of the war. It made me wonder if Mr. Asahi was one of the young men separated from his family and exiled to Ontario to work for subsistence wages on a farm, under harsh physical conditions. I have also wondered whether Mrs Asahi faced any criticism, overt or otherwise, when she ventured to establish a relationship with a Japanese-Canadian, at a time when the hostilities with Japan had barely ended and the atmosphere of distrust and discrimination was still strong. This mistreatment of Japanese Canadians and complete disregard of their civil rights is one of the few black marks on the Canadian record of human rights.

I had also established a rapport with the landlady's teenage daughter and with the British lady who shared the room with her. As part of her room and board, the British lady helped with household chores like cooking, cleaning, changing bed sheets, and doing laundry. Sometimes when she came to my room for the weekly changing of sheets, we would share a smoke and she would talk about how boring her job was or about going back home in the near future. She did not appear to have a boyfriend or any social life. The landlady's teenage daughter, on the other hand, did have a boyfriend, a class mate from her high school. However, the relationship was getting rocky, as I found out during our occasional chats over tea and cigarettes, because he was demanded a closer relationship then she was willing to offer. She must have finally refused his demands because the relationship ultimately came to an end, and I did not notice any new boyfriend on the scene. Since I had little personal knowledge or insights into the North American teen culture, during these chats I felt like a celibate Catholic Priest who was listening to marital woes of one of his parishioners. I treated her like a younger cousin, and sometimes invited her to accompany me to a movie or she would invite me to come along with her to the Laundromat to keep her company. On a few occasions, I succumbed to her request to buy her a half bottle of vodka, which she insisted that I share with her in the privacy of my room so that her parents would not discover her transgressions.

The landlord's son, was a sweet and polite boy, and like many Canadian boys his age, he was into ice hockey in a big way. He was always talking about his favourite hockey teams – the Toronto Maple Leafs and the Montreal Canadians, and his hockey heroes – Frank Mahovelich, Rocket Richard, Gordie Howe, Jean Beliveau and Boom Boom Geofrion. At that time, I knew very little about ice hockey or any of its related terminology; the only type of hockey I was familiar with was field hockey which is a popular sport in India. He was also the neighbourhood delivery boy for The Globe and Mail, the premier Canadian daily newspaper. It did not take much effort on his part to persuade me to become a subscriber. I did not have a television, or even a radio, in my room and needed some means of keeping current with local, national, and international news – although there was not much international coverage in The Globe, except for the usual Cold War happenings. It was nice to have a newspaper to read with my morning tea, though I never imagined that after almost half a century I would be reading The Globe and Mail with my morning tea, and watching the rush hour traffic on Avenue Road in Toronto. The next summer, my landlady was kind enough to provide me with an old AM/FM radio. Up until then, I had only heard Bollywood songs and some Indian classical music and had little appreciation of Western music – classical or popular. I mostly tuned into CHUM Radio Station and listened to popular hits of the time.

From my limited vantage point, I had not noticed any tension or conflict within the Asahi family - everything seemed to be quiet and serene. However, in the middle of one summer night, the tranquility was suddenly disturbed by sounds of loud and angry words from Mrs Asahi. A few days later when I noticed that the British young lady was no more boarding with us and enquired about her, I was told by Mrs Asahi that she was asked to leave because Mrs Asahi suspected that the lady in question was making moves on her husband. Mrs Asahi further expressed the opinion that the young lady was probably a nymphomaniac – a term she likely picked up from the highly popular novel Peyton Place, which had recently hit the market and exposed the scandal-ridden life in a fictitious small American town. I doubted that her highly subjective opinion was on the mark, but under the circumstances I did not have the heart to challenge her. However, after a short while things returned to normal and the minor tempest in the tea pot was a thing of the past.

I was glad that I was able to board with the Asahi family (rather than in a students' residence or private apartment) for the duration of my stay in Canada because it provided me with valuable insight into the day-to-day life of an urban, lower-middle class Canadian family. This close encounter with the Asahi family cleared many of my misconceptions about life in a Western family and made me realize that there is no significant difference between the basic needs and aspirations of middle-class families in the West or the East. Further, my landlady was kind enough to assume the role of Emily Post and gave me pointers on proper Western manners and etiquette which helped me greatly in navigating through the unfamiliar Canadian social landscape.

Date or not to date – a moral dilemma

As my first spring in Toronto blossomed, I started to notice the springtime rituals of young (and old) Canadians. Couples walked around holding hands with laughter and hope on their faces, lovers in tight embraces sitting on benches in city parks or the University grounds, and young ladies walking along Yonge Street in short shorts and flimsy halter tops. All these sights were completely unfamiliar to me and evoked instincts that had largely been dormant or more likely suppressed, as a result of the prevailing cultural attitudes in Indian society. In India, there was little interaction between the sexes, except between close family members, and little opportunity to gain knowledge or openly discuss matters related to sex and sexuality. As my hormones started responding to the Canadian spring scenes around me, I found myself being drawn towards taking advantage of the dating ritual and experience some closer contact with the opposite sex.

As I progressed through childhood, puberty and into early adulthood, I had a very patchy and uneven understanding of all things related to sex and human reproduction When I was growing up we were kept completely in the dark on such matters. Formal sex education classes were unheard of in those days, and neither my parents nor my older siblings ever talked to me about the so called 'facts of life'. The only time my father even came close to bringing up this topic was when he very obliquely and briefly spoke a few words about the harmful effects of masturbation, which he called 'hand practice', mainly because he was afraid that my skinny frame may have been caused by such activities.

When I was in grade six or seven, I recall having long discussions with my cousin about a mystery that had us completely baffled. It was a long established tradition in our family that every time a female in the house started her menstrual flow, she was quarantined and effectively became an untouchable person until the end of the menstrual flow. She was relegated to a corner of the house and excused from contributing to most daily household chores. She was not allowed in the kitchen or the common eating area and if any of us children accidentally touched her, we were to immediately take off all our clothes and leave them with her. We were then handed freshly washed clothes to put on. As children, we noticed that this change of status occurred very suddenly and we were mystified about the possible cause that triggered it. After about three days, the quarantined lady would have a ritual bath; wash her hair, her clothes, and any utensils she had used in the last three days. After changing into fresh clothes, she would be back in circulation. To growing and observant children like us, this was a mystery indeed. The only explanation we got from our reluctant elders was that the person had suddenly fallen ill, which, even at our age, we found rather lame and less than satisfactory.

Notwithstanding the fact that the *Kamasutra,* one of the oldest and most comprehensive treatises on love and lovemaking, was written in India early in the first millennium and that the temples at Khajuraho and Konarak and many other places in India, depict human sexuality explicitly and put it on display for everyone to see and admire, we were brought up in a highly puritan atmosphere and there was little downward communication about sexual matters. As we were growing up, any information, or misinformation we acquired on these topics was through 'boy talk' among our peers and by observing the copulation and birthing activities in the abundant animal life around us. Many of the misconceptions and large gaps in my knowledge in this area – for example, I did not know that women also masturbated and had orgasms – were only set right when I read Freud and Havelock Ellis when I was in my twenties.

While the hormonal pull was definitely a strong emotional motivator, from an intellectual perspective, I also felt that my experience of Canadian life would be incomplete if I entirely missed dating which is one of its most important social aspects. Every Canadian goes through the trials and tribulations of dating from a relatively early age, and it generally provides the preparation for selecting a life partner. In view of the fact that I had no plans for either staying or returning to Canada after finishing my studies, I was afraid of the complications that might result if my relationship with a Canadian girl became too serious. However, the real moral dilemma I faced was the fact that I was engaged to a girl from our community back in India, chosen by my family based on the compatibility of our horoscopes and family backgrounds. I was 29 years old and fast approaching the 'best before' date in the marriage market. I had consented to the proposal when I had no idea that I would soon be off to Canada for an extended period of time. The girl was studying home economics at a local girls' college and I had met her face-to-face for less than fifteen minutes at her home. After I arrived in Canada, I had little contact with her and was already starting to regret my decision, and I had started sending signals to this effect to my family. In spite of this dilemma, I decided to dip my toes into the unfamiliar waters, promising myself that I would stay in the shallows and avoid getting drawn towards the deep end. However, as

I soon found out, such an approach may be great in theory, but in the complex and unpredictable world of human relationships, it most often does not succeed.

The first girl I dated was a secretary in a downtown office whom I met when a group of us went on a trip to Caledon Farms arranged by FROS. She was not, and had never been, a university student but someone had told her that FROS was a good place to meet university-educated boys. She decided to try her luck, and the boy she ended up with was me, a novice at the game. A young well endowed blond, she was intelligent and knowledgeable, although not in an academic sense, and was essentially 'playing the field'. Our dates usually consisted of a movie and dinner or sometimes a visit to a dance club on Yonge Street. Her parents lived in a small house near the city centre and her father had a blue collar job in some factory. A few times when I met her parents, I could sense that they were not too happy to see their daughter going out with a person who was not their own type. Shortly after I met her, she moved to an apartment near Cabbage Town which she shared with another office colleague. Unfortunately, within a couple of months they were asked to vacate the apartment because they frequently hosted rather loud parties and the neighbours started to complain. She then moved into a room in one of the old houses near Bloor Street and soon after that I lost touch with her, as I was getting very busy with my thesis work. A year or so later, I accidentally met her on Yonge Street when she informed me that she had decided to marry an older, and richer Jewish man and that she was on her way to the Jewish Centre at the corner of Bloor and Spadina where she was taking instruction to convert to the Jewish faith in preparation for the upcoming wedding.

Over the next several months, I went out with a few more girls. One of whom was a nurse at a local hospital. She was a keen roller skater, and we frequently went to a nearby rink where she gave me my first lessons in roller skating. She also gave me some tips on contemporary dating protocols. For example, I did not know that in a restaurant, if the table is against a wall, the gentleman should take the chair facing the wall, and that when walking together on a sidewalk, the gentleman should walk on the side closer to the road – it seems the latter custom was established before the advent of indoor plumbing, in order to protect the lady from the contents of chamber pots being emptied from upper storey balconies..

The point of inflection

So far my ventures into dating had been reasonably casual and I had avoided getting drawn into deeper waters. However, things took a different turn when I met my next date, moving the trajectory of two lives into uncharted and unanticipated directions. In the spring of 1963, Swaroop (one of my Indian friends at the University) was dating a Japanese-Canadian student named Marjorie. Marjorie was an active participant in FROS activities and I had met her on many occasions and liked her. She had a summer job at what was then called The Ontario Crippled Children's Centre (OCCC) on Bayview Avenue near Sunnybrook Hospital. Marjorie decided to arrange a blind date for me with her immediate supervisor, a nursing graduate working as a play therapist with the handicapped children. Either Marjorie used some very persuasive arguments to convince her to meet me and go on a blind double date or she may have caught her at a vulnerable moment. Anyway, the die was cast and on the evening of June 6th, 1963. Swaroop and Marjorie drove me to 142 Bedford Road and I rang the bell with anticipation and excitement, mixed with some trepidation, waiting for the first glimpse of my mystery date. Finally, the door opened and there was Miss MARGARET Ruth Windrem – a very attractive, well proportioned girl of average height with dark hair and dark eyes wearing a beautiful yellow silk dress. After formal introductions, we drove off for dinner at a popular Chinese restaurant on Dundas Street.

Marjorie was quite knowledgeable about Chinese food and she made sure that we had a sumptuous feast. When we finished dinner, it was bright daylight outside and the evening was still young. We decided to spend the rest of the evening near the lake where we could enjoy the cool breeze. After making a detour to allow the ladies to change into more casual clothes, we went to the lakeshore near the Exhibition Grounds. We had a very pleasant time watching the sailboats on the lake and the sunset with the Toronto Islands as a backdrop. It was almost midnight when Swaroop and Marjorie dropped Margaret and I at her residence. It was a warm summer night and we decided to sit on the front steps and get better acquainted on various levels, including: social, intellectual and, to a limited extent, physical. We had agreed to meet again the next evening for a quick meal and a trip to High Park for a leisurely stroll. That evening, High Park was full of people, taking advantage of the fine summer weather. Margaret still teases me about our walk in High Park that day because whenever I saw persons who looked as if they were from India, coming towards us, I would let go of her hand and pretend that the two of us were just casual acquaintances. I guess I had not yet overcome my long-held inhibitions about public displays of intimacy.

For my part, I don't think that it was 'love at first sight', but it certainly was 'attraction at first sight'. I was drawn to Margaret on all the important levels – social, intellectual, and physical – and was keen to spend time with her and learn more about her world view, her family and her values. As the summer progressed, we started spending more and more time together. We saw Shirley McLane and Jack Lemon in Irma la Douce, Barbara Hamilton in person in That Hamilton Woman, and attended a Bach concert at the Eaton College Street Theatre. We spent an evening listening to calypso music and limbo dancing on a boat tour around the harbour. We went on picnics at Ramsay Park and Edwards Gardens We double-dated with Bob and Elaine, Swaroop and his girl of the day, and with Paloma, a Spanish colleague of Margaret's, whose boyfriend owned a convertible. More often than not, we found ourselves in some coffee house in Yorkville listening to folk music or spending the evening in Margaret's room watching television and getting to know each other better. Sometimes these evenings lasted until the wee hours. It seems that Margaret's Dutch landlord, who, with his wife, occupied the ground floor of the large house, was not too happy with these late night visits. One night when I was leaving, he confronted me in the mode of an overprotective parent. Margaret had to set him right the next day, making it clear that he had no *locus standi* to interfere with her personal life.

Very soon I learned about Margaret's rural Ontario background, her immediate family and the network of relatives she grew up with. She was born on a farm on the outskirts of Lindsay, Ontario, a town with a population of about 10,000, in the Kawartha Lakes area. Her father came from an Irish Protestant background and was one of a large family. Her mother had a Scottish background and her father was an early adherent of the religious movement that evolved into the Jehovah's Witnesses. Margaret had two siblings an older brother and a younger brother, both of whom were married and had young children. Margaret had attended a one-room public school which you could see from her farm. When she graduated from the Lindsay Collegiate Institute, she was one of the top students. However, at that time the opportunities open to women who wished to pursue a career were limited to nursing, teaching or secretarial work – the woman's liberation movement was barely on the horizon. Margaret opted for nursing, graduated from the Atkinson School of Nursing at the Toronto Western Hospital, and later obtained a Diploma in Public Health Nursing from the University of Toronto.

Margaret was working as a public health nurse with the Victorian Order of Nurses in Toronto when her father suddenly passed away from a heart attack, around the same time that I had lost my mother. She decided to return to Lindsay to help and support her grieving mother and was considering a job offer there. However, her mother decided to pass the farm on to her older son and to move to Toronto to live with her two widowed sisters. The three moved into an apartment on Roehampton Avenue and Margaret returned to Toronto to start working at the Ontario Crippled Children's Centre. Soon, I was a frequent visitor at her mother's apartment, enjoying afternoon tea and pleasant dinners. I liked Margaret's mother who sometimes reminded me of my grandmother, in that they were both good at telling stories about the trials and tribulations of relatives and neighbours living in a close-knit community. I also met her two brothers and their families who often came down to visit their mother

By the end of my second summer in Toronto, Margaret and I were seeing each other almost every day and spending a lot of time together. As our daughter would say, we had become an 'item'. However, when our daughter told us that she and her boyfriend, whom she later married, were now an 'item', she also indicated that this new status entitled her to cohabit with him. In our case, the times were different and the sexual revolution had yet to arrive. This drastic change in social attitudes towards sex was heralded by the widespread use of the birth control pill and the rapidly gaining strength of the feminist movement. Although Western society had shed many of its puritanical attitudes from the Victorian era, in 1963, remnants of Victorian morality remained in 'Toronto the Good' and in most of English Canada, as well. Archaic liquor laws and Lord's Day restrictions were still in effect, and the appearance of 'propriety' was paramount in relationships with members of the opposite sex. Although Margaret and I were now an 'item', spending a night together or living together as a couple before marriage was not an option. On a few occasions during out courtship, this led to some degree of inconvenience and frustration. However, although we recognized that many of these attitudes verged on being hypocritical, we had to respect the social norms of the day. Times have certainly changed since then – not only did our children live together with their partners for significant periods before they married them, but many of our friends and relatives, our age and older, are cohabiting with their partners, openly, honestly, and happily.

Over the summer and fall, I met many of Margaret's close and not-so-close relatives, including various uncles, aunts and cousins scattered in and around the Lindsay area. I was frequently invited to the family farm and attended the annual Lindsay Fair where I experienced my first ride on a roller coaster. In early fall, we spent a week at a cottage on Sturgeon Lake near Lindsay – properly chaperoned, of course, by Margaret's mother, two aunts, and two sister-in-laws who took turns as necessary. Spending time at the lakeshore cottage was one more experience of typical Canadian life style and a very pleasant and enjoyable one.

I spent my third Christmas in Canada at the farm and finally was exposed not only to the Christmas spirit that is part of a family gathering, but also to the beauty of the landscape at Christmas time in rural Canada. With fields covered in snow as far as the eye could see, interrupted only by the occasional farmhouse lit with coloured Christmas lights, the scene and the atmosphere evoked the true sense of 'peace and goodwill' associated with the Christmas season. Compared to this, in retrospect, my first Christmas in Canada had been a bit of a letdown. I had only recently arrived in Canada and had a very hazy understanding of how Christmas is celebrated here. Major religious events in India are called festivals, not holidays, such as the *Diwali* festival, *Holi* festival, *Eid* festival, etc. These festivals are celebrated with family, friends, neighbours and even strangers, all in a more public setting. Lots of people are out and about greeting one another, visiting temples or mosques and attending cultural events (music, dancing), and visiting special displays designed for the occasion. Therefore, expecting that the streets would be full of people celebrating the most important religious event in the Christian calendar, I decided to walk around College Street and Spadina Avenue on Christmas night. To my surprise, I found that there was an eerie silence all around, with hardly any pedestrians and very few cars on the streets. By the time my second Christmas came around, I had a better understanding of Canadian Christmas rituals. I sent Christmas greeting cards and bought gifts for the department secretaries and for my landlady and her children. In turn, my landlady invited me to join her family for a typical Christmas dinner, consisting of a roast turkey with all the trimmings.

Although I belonged to a different race, a different religion, and a different culture, I was greatly impressed and gratified that I never encountered even a trace of discomfort at anytime during my frequent contacts with Margaret's family and the people around them. I give great credit to the residents of this part of rural Canada, who probably had never had much contact with a South

Asian person, for their spirit of generosity and inclusiveness, and even more to the members of Margaret's immediate family who displayed such unquestioning trust in her values and confidence in her judgement.

A conditional proposal

As the Christmas of 1963 approached, so did the end of my study period in Canada and the expected date of my departure. It also brought the future of my relationship with Margaret to the forefront. As I had come to know her over the past six months, I was increasingly attracted to her and the attraction was more than just physical. I was also greatly impressed by her keen intelligence, her uncommonly generous spirit, and her unwavering empathy towards people – especially towards children. I felt that I was falling in love with her – not the Hollywood/Bollywood version of love, but a more realistic version that happens when two adults strongly feel that they are compatible on many levels and can build a stable and meaningful life together for themselves and their children. After a long and difficult inner conflict, I finally decided that I would consider the possibility of us getting married provided Margaret would be prepared to come to India (possibly never to return) and live in a country with a radically different social, cultural and economic environment, and provided I could persuade my family to accept, and hopefully, welcome her into the family as my bride. I strongly felt that these conditions and commitments were necessary for the success and stability of our cross-cultural marriage, particularly if we were to live in India. Another hurdle that I had to resolve before I could proceed was, of course, to formally end my engagement to the girl in India.

To make sure that Margaret received a realistic picture of life in contemporary India, I provided her with as much information as I could on my family background, our Hindu religious beliefs and practices, cultural and economic conditions in the country and my own daily routine at the Engineering College where I taught and lived. I explained that compared to the West, my life in India was rather simple and primitive. For example, such conveniences as electric/gas stoves and ovens, refrigerators, washers and dryers, telephones, televisions, and motorized vehicles were not part of my lifestyle. In my ancestral village, electricity and running water were still things of the future. Perhaps I painted a picture that appeared more unappealing than the reality. After all, most middle-class households in India employed one or more servants to take care of everyday housekeeping chores, such as cooking, cleaning, laundering and gardening.

As my departure date drew closer, one evening in a coffee house in Yorkville, having once again gone over the conditions of life in India, I asked Margaret the following question, "If I were to ask you to marry me and move to India to live there, would you say yes?" Her answer was an immediate and emphatic YES. The proposal was still somewhat hypothetical and tentative because I wanted to confirm her willingness to make such a life-altering commitment before subjecting my family to making an equally momentous and difficult decision. To welcome an unknown, white, Christian Canadian lady into the family, entirely on my say so, would be a pioneering step in the annals of our family, our community, and our entire social and professional circle. Having received Margaret's positive answer, I would be leaving her behind with the fervent hope that things would work out back in India and she would come to India to dress as an Indian bride for the second time – this time for real. She had already dressed up as an Indian bride in a 'Brides of India' pageant arranged by the Indian community in Toronto as part of a *Diwali* celebration.

The last few weeks before my departure for India in January of 1964 passed quickly. The management and staff where I was an intern held a farewell lunch and gave me a number of nice gifts. The Canadian government arranged for the packing and shipping of my personal effects, including the extra large suitcase I had brought in the hope of filling it with all kinds of Western goods. In the end, all I took back to impress my family and friends was an Omega watch, a Canon camera and a pair of Levi jeans. Margaret decided to accompany me to Ottawa and then to Montreal to see me off. My friend, Swaroop, drove us to Union Station for the overnight train to Ottawa where we stayed with Bob and Elaine in their little apartment in Lower Town. The next day I met my contact at the federal government building on Parliament Hill to pick up my airline tickets and thank him for his assistance and advice during my stay. The next day, we took the train to Montreal where Margaret's cousin and his wife met us. He was an executive with Texaco Canada and had a house in Beaconsfield neighbourhood near the airport, where we stayed the night – in separate bedrooms, of course. My BOAC flight to London the next evening was rescheduled due to inclement weather, which gave us the bonus of an extra evening together. Next morning Margaret gave me a goodbye and a *bon voyage* kiss, at the departure gate to the applause of the gate attendants. I had to spend an extra night in London and another in Dubai because of missed connections and technical problems. Finally, on a cold and foggy morning, I arrived back at the New Delhi airport ending my first close encounter with the West and thinking of the hopes and hurdles that lay ahead.

INDIA (1932 – 1961)

****

CHAPTER 3

Childhood in a small Indian town

I was born into a Brahmin family in 1932 at Jabalpur, a city of about half a million inhabitants in the Central part of India. I was the youngest son and the fifth child in a family of four brothers and three sisters. At the time, my father was employed as a public school teacher in a school operated by a large manufacturing facility called the Gun Carriage Factory owned and operated by the British Indian Army. The Gun Carriage Factory is still going strong, but now instead of producing gun carriages, it manufactures heavy-duty trucks and jeeps for the Indian Army. The school was primarily meant for the children of factory employees, who were also provided with residential facilities in its vicinity. I was born in one of these three-room, government-issue houses. The birth would have been assisted by my grandmother and a midwife with no formal training, except that she belonged to the midwifery caste with the trade handed down to her through generations. Following our family tradition, my mother would have been quarantined for ten days after the birth, and fed a special diet rich in iron and laced with dried fruit and nuts and herbal ingredients such as turmeric and dried ginger to ward off infections. Twice a day, she and the baby would be given a massage by a female masseuse to tone up and strengthen their muscles. After ten days, she would have had a ritual bath in hot water containing herbs and would not be back to normal household duties for another four weeks. Following the prevailing practice, my horoscope was cast soon after my birth and astrologers were consulted about the broad aspects of my adult personality and future prospects. I am told that after examining my horoscope and the underside of my feet, the astrologer divined that I was not likely to sit still in one place and would travel extensively. Given the modest circumstances in which we were living, I do not think much credence was given to this seemingly outlandish prediction.

At the time I was born, the British Raj was well entrenched in India and the sun was still shining brightly over the British Empire. However, signs of looming troubles were on the horizon. Mahatma Gandhi's non-violent struggle to dislodge British rule from India was gaining momentum. Many of the leaders of Gandhi's All India Congress Party were in jail for non-violent resistance to some of the unjust burdens placed on India's poor masses. At the same time, North America was moving towards a deepening economic depression that caused untold suffering and brought Roosevelt's leadership into sharp focus with his New Deal. Germany and Japan were laying the groundwork for another confrontation leading up to World War II, which would ultimately change the geopolitics of the entire world.

Jabalpur, birthplace of Snooker

Jabalpur is similar to scores of medium-sized cities in India, mostly unplanned and congested except for the areas that were inhabited by the British administrators and the senior members of the British Indian Army. In India, these areas are generally referred as 'cantonments'. The cantonment was well planned and had cricket and soccer fields, civil and army clubs, parks with bandstands, and large bungalows on spacious grounds, each with open verandas and separate accommodation for scores of servants. Jabalpur's only claim-to-fame is the fact that the game of Snooker originated at the Narmada Club located there. The city is situated in the vicinity of the Narmada River, one of India's many holy rivers. The river originates in the Vindhya Range of mountains east of Jabalpur and flows east to west all the way to the Arabian Sea. A few miles from the city, the river cuts through a gorge of white soapstone which is a tourist attraction called marble rocks. A slow boat ride through the gorge on a moonlit night is a beautiful and romantic experience. Tourists also come to Jabalpur to start the 80 km journey to the wildlife sanctuary at Kanha-Kesli where they can ride an elephant into the sanctuary and see tigers, leopards, and other wild animals in their natural habitat. A lot of low hills are scattered around the city, as well as a number of small lakes some of which are often used for harvesting water chestnuts.

Early moves

When I was still a toddler, we moved to Timarni, a smaller town about 150 km west of Jabalpur where my father had accepted another teaching position.

I was too young to have any recollections of my early childhood in Jabalpur. However, I do have some fleeting memories of our short stay in Timarni. We lived in a large house that was built on a very high plinth so that one had to climb almost ten steps to reach the front door. It had a large courtyard at the back, ending in a barn-like room used for our milking cows. The courtyard had a large well on one side and a tall guava tree on the other which was a favourite place for my brothers to climb and pick the fruits. I vaguely recall travelling on a train with our family to attend my older sister's wedding. I think she was only sixteen at the time and her marriage was arranged to a young man recommended by one of my aunts.

The road in front of our house was on the route to the town's cremation grounds. I would often watch funeral processions going by, with a dead body covered in a white sheet on a makeshift bier being carried by four men on their shoulders. The procession was led by a few musicians beating drums and a relative carrying an earthen pot with live coals to light the funeral pyre. At frequent intervals, the people in the processions would throw a few coins which were collected by a throng of urchins who would follow the procession. We were strictly forbidden to pick up those coins – we were told that only boys from the untouchable community were supposed to do it.

Our stay in Timarni did not last very long. When I was about five years old, our family returned permanently to our ancestral home, located in Hatta, a very small town – practically a village, about 150 km northwest of Jabalpur. The sudden move was precipitated by a medical emergency that my father suffered while visiting the ancestral home during the summer vacation. He had been visiting his younger sister who lived in a village about 15 km away, and he walked home from there, arriving back before noon. To cool off, he made himself a drink called *thandai* (a cooling drink) which is made by mixing water, milk, sugar, caramelized rose petals and a paste consisting of almonds, raisins, anise, cardamoms, and poppy seeds. More often than not, the paste is also spiked with marijuana leaves, giving the drinker a mild high, although I do not know if this was the case here. After drinking a large glass of this drink, my father started to walk towards the local river for a bath and swim. En route, he suddenly felt dizzy and passed out on the street. Fortunately, an Ayurvedic doctor was available nearby and was able to revive him. The episode frightened my father and he asked his employers for an extended leave to make sure that the problem was not systemic. The leave was denied, so he decided to resign and move back permanently to the ancestral home. He also decided to follow a very regimented and health-conscious lifestyle for the rest of his life to ward of any recurrence of the scary episode. After settling in our ancestral home, my father left it only once, for medical treatment until he passed away at the age of 84. I spent my childhood years in Hatta until, just shy of my fourteenth birthday when I had to move to a larger city to continue my education.

Our town and the region

When we moved to Hatta, it had a population of about 7,000 inhabitants. In British India, the hierarchy of the British administration was based on provinces which were further subdivided into Districts (counties), and Tahsils (sub-counties). In this hierarchical structure, Hatta was a Tahsil in the District of Saugor in the province of Central Provinces and Berar. Besides the various provinces directly administered by the British Governor General at New Delhi, there were also more than 500 princely states whose Indian rulers (Rajas, Maharaja, Nawabs) owed allegiance to the British Sovereign through the Viceroy - a parallel role assigned to the Governor General. The Viceroy exerted control over the princely states through so called Political Agents who kept a tight reign on Rajas and Maharajas to ensure that they were suitably aligned with the Royal wishes. After India gained independence, most of the princely states became an integral part of India.

Historically, the region where our hometown is located is called *Bundelkhand*, the region of *Bundels*; because a warrior dynasty called *Bundels* ruled the region for a number of centuries before the arrival of the British Raj. The local language, *Bundelkhandi* is one of the major dialects of Hindi, the language spoken in most of Northern India. This is the region where the famous Khajuraho temples, built between the 11th and 13th century, with their aesthetically exquisite and sexually explicit sculptures, are located. It is also the region where the term 'thugs' originated, to describe the widespread network of robbers who plied their nefarious trade in this area for over a century. They claimed to be devotees of the Hindu goddess *Kali* and indulged in ritual murder and robbery by joining groups of unsuspecting travellers and strangling them, using a large handkerchief with a silver coin tied at one end. The practice was called *thuggee* which means 'the practice of deceiving' in the local language. It was finally eliminated by the then British administration around 1830 AD, and a bunch of thugs were captured and publicly hanged in the main market square at Jabalpur. John Masters' novel, The Deceivers, provides an interesting and illuminating narrative on the practice of *thuggee* and a British administrator's adventures in pursuing the thugs and eliminating the practice. The British officer who is actually credited with leading the campaign against the practice of *thuggee* was William Henry Sleeman of the Indian Political Service, and the town of Sleemanabad, which is about 100 km from Hatta, is named after him.

The town of Hatta is located on a high plateau on the eastern bank of Sunar River which flows south to north. The river is about 200 meters wide and the town has a number of *ghaats* or series of stone steps to reach the water which are similar to the famous *ghaats* of Varanasi along the Ganges River. The various *ghaats* along the river bank which are crowned by many temples provide panoramic views of the town from the far shore of the river. Since the town is located on a high plateau, the numerous wells within the town usually dried up during the summer and the river is the only source of water for the town dwellers in the dry season. Carrying large pots of water over all the steep steps and delivering them to households in town was a daunting task for the water carriers. The northern and southern boundaries of Hatta are roughly defined by two large streams that flow into the river and a single-lane paved road marks the eastern boundary on which buses ply to and from the surrounding towns. In the southwest corner of the town, there is an old abandoned fort, and as a child, my friends and I spent many hours exploring the innumerable nooks and crannies inside, as well as the thick ramparts and fortifications marking the periphery of the abandoned fort.

Not far from the fort is a small Daak Bungalow (Rest House) located on a promontory at the confluence of the river and a large stream. The chosen location of the Daak Bungalow provides a panoramic view of the river and the town below. These Daak Bungalows were built by the British Administration so that its officials would be ensured of comfortable accommodations when they travelled on their tours of inspection. Such facilities can be found in towns and cities across India, and are generally located on scenic spots at some distance from the local population. The Daak Bungalow in our town was staffed by a *khansama* (cook) a *chowkidaar* (watchman), a *maali* (gardener) and a *jamadaar* (cleaner), who maintained the facility and looked after the daily needs of the visiting *sahibs*. The jamadaar who belonged to the untouchable caste was responsible, among other cleaning jobs, for collecting, emptying and cleaning the bathroom commode (some times referred as the 'thunder box' in the vernacular) after each use. The colonial era thunder box was simply a straight back chair with an appropriate sized hole in the middle and a detachable enamel pot underneath to capture the output of the *sahib's* business. It is a pity that in recent years, many of these colonial era landmarks (especially in small towns) have fallen prey to poor oversight and shoddy maintenance and like many of the colonial era institutions, their glory days are behind them

Hatta has dozens of Hindu and Jain temples, a Muslim mosque and a prayer ground (where Muslims gather for special prayers on the festival of Eid), and a small Christian church. When I was growing up, the educational facilities were limited to two boys' primary schools (grades 1-4), one girls' primary school and a co-ed middle school (grades 5-8). In terms of medical facilities, there was a small government hospital, actually a dispensary, run by a licensed medical practitioner, as well as a handful of private practitioners of Ayurvedic medicine. The hospital doctor was the jack-of-all medicine-related trades and tackled medical, surgical, and dental complaints using his limited professional training and the meagre facilities and resources available to him. Most of the medications he dispensed consisted of liquid concoctions or balms that he mixed himself and patients received them free-of-charge as long as they brought their own bottles or suitable containers to carry them home. The doctor also performed post mortems whenever there was a suspicious death within the sub-county's jurisdiction. The post mortem house was located outside the town boundary and consisted of a single room with good ventilation inside a walled and secure compound. Once, when I was home during vacations from the university, the doctor who was a friend invited me to come along for a post mortem on a young woman killed by her husband for suspected adultery. The experience was not a pleasant one and it probably contributed to my reluctance to study medicine.

There were two open air markets, one each at the south and the north ends of the town, with the open areas surrounded by permanent shops selling groceries, clothing and sweets, as well as by tailors, silversmiths, iron and brass workers and other artisans. The open area was mainly used by fresh vegetable, fruit and flower sellers. The larger of the two markets was used for bi-weekly market days when people from the surrounding villages came down to sell their produce and buy household necessities not available in their own small villages. As a child, going to the small market every morning with my father to buy fresh vegetables and fruits was a pleasant and exciting part of the daily routine – especially observing the fine art of bargaining displayed by both sides in coming to a mutually agreeable transaction.

The sub-county administration offices, including the magisterial courts and the police station, were located in the southwest corner of the town near the abandoned fort. The middle school, built in 1905, with its extensive playgrounds, marked the southeast and the cremation grounds on the river bank delineated the northwest boundary. There were also a number of good sized man made ponds on the outskirts of the town which were fed by the monsoon rains and they usually dried up in the summer. However, they were quite suitable for growing water chestnuts and lotus flowers during the winter months. The ponds were also great for swimming during the rainy season when the rain-swollen river became too dangerous to swim in.

Our community

Our family was part of a very small community called *Khedawal* Brahmins who migrated to Hatta from the western Indian State of Gujarat some time in the late 18th or early 19th century. The families originated from a district in Gujarat called *Kheda* which has little historical significance except that it was the site of Mahatma Gandhi's early experiments in non-violent resistance against the British Raj. In 1918, Gandhi and his close lieutenant Vallabhbhai Patel launched a successful campaign for the fair and humane treatment of drought-stricken farmers in this place whose farms and property were being confiscated by the British administration for tax defaults. Our community of expatriate Gujarati Brahmins in the town consisted of a few dozen families who had little contact with their place of origin. However, over the years they were able to maintain their linguistic identity and most of their social customs and religious rituals, as well as their cuisine. The language spoken in our home was mostly Gujarati, and as a child I was reasonably proficient in it and could read the script, which is similar to the Hindi script. The following folklore is commonly accepted as the rationale for the sudden *en masse* migration of the small Brahmin community from the western province of Gujarat to the far away central Indian town of Hatta:

It is said that a certain gentleman, Mr Dave (pronounced *the-way*) from *Kheda* in Gujarat secured a high administrative position in a princely state with its capital located in Panna which is about 100 km north of Hatta. One day while on his daily walk he came across a group of children playing with some shiny pebbles. He happened to pick one up and immediately recognized that it was no ordinary pebble, but a raw uncut diamond. He bought the pebbles for a nominal payment and contracted the children to collect as many such pebbles as they could find and bring them to him in exchange for coins. It is believed that the diamonds had come to the surface in the local area and were easy pickings. (Diamonds are still occasionally found in Panna, though now they have to be mined.) After a while, Mr Dave had collected enough raw diamonds and was afraid that the news would leak out and the ruler of the state would confiscate his treasure. So, one night he slipped away with his treasure and finally ended up in the town of Hatta which was outside the jurisdictional boundaries of the princely state. In a short period, he became very prosperous However, he and his immediate family felt lonely being so far away from their home and culture and he decided to entice some of his relatives and friends from his home in Gujarat to come and join him with the promise that they would be well looked after on their arrival. So his poor relatives and friends trekked down to this far away town in an alien territory.

Mr Dave was true to his promise, and looked after the new arrivals well. He served them daily meals at his residence until they were settled in their own homes and he bought them farmland in the surrounding villages so that they could earn their living. Some of the families that migrated to Hatta brought their favourite gods and goddesses, not only in spirit but also in substance. For example, my father's ancestors and a few other families, brought their *kuldevi* (a female deity belonging to the family or clan), which consisted of a clay statue about three feet high representing the goddess *Durga* who is one of the manifestations of Lord Shiva's wife in Hindu mythology. The deity is still an important and integral part of our family and currently resides in our private temple. Every morning and evening, a family member has to go to the temple to conduct *pooja*, a brief ritual for the deity, and invariably young neighbourhood children gather around to share the *prasad*, the food blessed by the goddess, which generally consists of a few sugar crystals.

Thus a small group of *Khedawal* Brahmins from Gujarat were planted in a small town in Central India. It was a small community with about a dozen Gujarati last names, such as: Dave, Pandya, Bhatt, Mehta, Selot and Joshi. The original immigrant families stayed in Hatta, establishing themselves as a distinct community and earning their living as landowners and managers.

A few members of the community who developed skills in diamond cutting, polishing and merchandising later decided to relocate to places in North and South India, to be closer to many of the larger and wealthier princely states which represented the major markets for diamonds and diamond jewellery. My mother's family, who were in the diamond business, moved to a city in South India, and some other families moved to Varanasi in North India. My maternal grandfather was the last member of my immediate family to be in the business of marketing upscale diamond jewellery from his South Indian location, but some of the community members who moved to Varanasi are still in the business. For example, the Pandyas and Joshis of Varanasi are significant players in the diamond trade in places like Mumbai and New York.

As time passed and the original community grew, more members of the community moved to surrounding towns and cities which provided better opportunities for their livelihoods. Further, as the British administration started to expand their Western educational institutions, originally to recruit lower ranks for their civil service, the community readily embraced the opportunities for learning – as descendants of the Brahmin community, learning and the pursuit of knowledge was their defining vocation. As an example, 25 percent of the children who graduated with me from middle school were from our community, although the population of our community in the town was relatively miniscule. I believe that the current households of our community in the town represent less than half the original settler households. Most of the community, which has multiplied significantly, is now concentrated in urban centres such as Bhopal and Jabalpur in the state, and dispersed across the country and around the globe.

Our neighbourhood

Our ancestral home was located in the northwest part of the town, and in those days, was the last house on the street. Our neighbours represented different castes, communities, and economic levels. For example, our neighbours across the street were Muslims engaged in producing and selling fluffed cotton used as filling for warm comforters and jackets. Behind them was a family of untouchables who removed night soil and cleaned toilets, and not far from our house was a colony of leather workers, also of the untouchable caste because they disposed of dead cattle and consumed the meat from the carcasses. Other castes/communities represented in the neighbourhood included cotton weavers, milk men, water carriers, bangle makers and sellers, vegetable farmers and a handful of other (indigenous) Brahmins.

Boys and girls from all these diverse households always played together, with the usual gender separation, and developed lasting friendships across caste and religious boundaries. However, certain long-established protocols had to be maintained. Only friends from my own specific community were allowed to go into the interior living areas of our house, and we were not allowed to have any direct physical contact with children from the untouchable households who some times played with us. If this happened accidentally, I had to immediately go home, discard and leave my clothes for washing and have a bath. As children, we rarely questioned these strange rules of social behaviour, and if we did, they were explained to us as a matter of good hygiene, in the case of untouchables, or as a matter of division of labour and the long-term survival of different trades, in the case of the separation of castes and communities. With the "One Person, One Vote" principle of today's democratic India, as well as the increasing urbanization and introduction of strong affirmative action in education and employment, these social barriers are slowly breaking down. By sheer numbers, the communities on the lower rungs of the caste system who call themselves *Dalits* (oppressed) have gained significant clout within the Indian political system. The *Dalits* are very vigilant in ensuring that they are not deprived of the rights and privileges afforded to them by the Indian Constitution. To illustrate that things are progressing on this front, beyond my own pioneering steps, a number of my nieces and nephews have opted for intra-caste life partners. However, the pace of change is quite slow and this type of discrimination is still pervasive in rural India.

Our ancestral home

The house of my childhood was a large collection of many rooms, courtyards, patios, and entrances. One entered the front courtyard from the main south door. This led to a covered patio or veranda which was the main living room –very few guests were allowed beyond the front veranda unless they were members of the family or close friends of the family. There was little furniture on the veranda, except for a swing on one end and a rug with a large bolster on the other – this was my father's sitting area where he did the daily accounts, read the newspaper and conducted his household and farming-related business. There were two small rooms on either side of the veranda. One was designated as my grandmother's room and the second was a sort of study with a chair and a desk which I often used to do my homework during my student days. This room opened onto a small patio which was a favourite place for me to sleep during the hot summer nights – especially because I could stay up late into the night talking to my friends without my parents' knowledge. The veranda led into a large room which was mainly used as a bedroom by my father and other family members. The large bedroom had a number of cupboards built into the thick walls which were used to store valuables (jewellery, silver utensils, etc.) and important documents. On one side of the large room was a smaller room used for storing clothes and bed linens. On the other end a set of steps led to a large airy room on the upper floor with windows on all sides. This second floor room was also used for sleeping and as a gathering place when all of my brothers were home on vacations.

The kitchen and eating area was a long narrow room equipped with a two-burner, homemade, wood-burning contraption, called a *chulah*, made with clay, and a coal- burning brazier, both used for cooking. For meals, we sat cross-legged on low wooden stools and our strictly vegetarian food was served on round brass plates called *thalis* and small brass bowls called *katories*. There were two more rooms on either side of the kitchen, one of which was used for storing food staples and the other as a prayer room. The kitchen led into a second, larger courtyard with more rooms around it, one for housing our milking cows and buffalos, one for storing hay and wood, and another for storing food grains from our farms. In the dry seasons, a corner of this courtyard was also used for cooking and eating evening meals.

There was a large, deep well near the back corner of the house which was the primary source of water for the neighbourhood except during the two hottest months of the year when it completely dried up. It was a common sight in the morning and evening to see ladies balancing large containers of water on their heads as they carried them back home. The well was also the place where the neighbourhood women gathered to exchange news and gossip. Beyond the well was a monument to a woman who had committed *sati* - a practice in which a Hindu widow ostensibly proved her eternal love for her husband by making the ultimate sacrifice by throwing herself on his funeral pyre. It seems that in the past the practice was not uncommon in the region because similar monuments could be found on the outskirts of the town. In many instances however, helpless Hindu widows were being pressured, forced or doped into the cruel act by the

63

people around them, for their own selfish reasons. The ghastly practice was fortunately abolished in the 19th century by the British administration

Our family

I do not know very much about my father's side of our family except that my grandfather was a primary school teacher and had an older brother who lived with him all of his life. The family was extremely poor, so much so that the two brothers had a hard time persuading households in our community to give them a daughter in marriage. While the older brother never got married, my grandfather managed to marry my grandmother, who was only six years old, while he was at the ripe old age of thirty. The story goes that at some point my grandmother's father made a promise to my grandfather's family that if he had a daughter he would give her in marriage to my grandfather and it seems he was true to his word. My grandmother was a large, big boned woman, with a phenomenal appetite. She had her first child before she was 16 and was a great-great grandmother after living for over a hundred years. She had eight children, my father being the second child. Married into a poor household with no external help or support, she was busy with housework from early in the morning, grinding the grain for the daily bread, to late at night. To ensure that my father, as an infant, and his older sister, a toddler, would have a long nap during the day, she fed them small amounts of opium so that she could finish her household chores without having to attend to them.

It was a stroke of luck when my mother's relatively rich family agreed to accept my father as a son-in-law. The substantial wealth that my mother brought with her as her dowry not only boosted the financial status and lifestyle of my father's family, but also enabled my father to get a decent education. This infusion of wealth allowed our family to buy farmland in surrounding villages and to renovate and substantially enlarge our ancestral home. The family was able to climb a few rungs on the socioeconomic ladder, moving from being very poor to middle-class with a reasonably comfortable, although not lavish, lifestyle.

As long as my father was alive, daily life in our home revolved around his routine. He was the patriarch of the family and his wishes were almost always final. The only person he deferred to occasionally was his older sister who was also a strong personality and the matriarch of her own large family. At 6'4", weighing over 200 pounds, my father was a large man and had an impressive presence. The fainting episode that ultimately resulted in his decision to return permanently to our ancestral home, affected his concerns about his physical health. He placed little faith in Western or Eastern medicine, so he decided that the only way to ward off serious illness was by following a strict daily regime and healthy lifestyle, which included a very simple and restricted diet. His daily routine was almost etched in stone, and I do not recall him altering it unless some unusual circumstance, such as severe illness or a family emergency interfered with it.

Public school days

When our family returned to our ancestral home in Hatta, I was about five years old, and shortly thereafter I accompanied my mother on an extended visit to her parents' house in South India. My maternal grandparents had passed away by then, and my maternal uncle had left the jewellery business. He made his living from the farms, fruit orchards, and coconut groves he had inherited. He had six sons of varying ages, and I remember having a fabulous time during the visit, enjoying the South Indian cuisine which was mostly rice rather than wheat, and mostly coffee rather than tea, gorging on sweet mangoes from my uncle's orchards, and roaming around with my cousins. One thing that sticks in my memory from the visit is the awful taste of warm castor oil that I was force-fed as part of the purging ritual that all of the children had to endure at least once a month. At the end of the summer after our return from the south, I was enrolled in the local primary school to begin my long and uneven journey towards higher education and a professional career.

The local primary school was a five minute walk from my home. The town council, which had very limited funds, operated the school, so the facilities were very basic. The building consisted of three classrooms, with verandas extending along the three rooms on both sides. Since the school had classes from grades one to four, one of the classes had to be held in a veranda and as luck would have it, every year my class happened to be assigned the veranda. The sum total of the furniture consisted of a single table, and a few chairs for teachers and four blackboards. The school had no sports facilities or programs.

The students sat on long narrow *dhurries* that were rolled out every morning and rolled back at the end of classes. We had to bring our own books, reusable writing media, such as slate boards, and paper, pen and ink. All students and teachers were required to wear some type of head covering (various types of caps) during school hours, perhaps as an acknowledgement that we were in a learning institution. I wore a cap made of home-spun cotton that is generally called a 'Gandhi cap', although Gandhi never wore one. If we forgot to wear a cap to school, we were sent home to get one before we could be admitted to class. Most of the instruction was by rote, although it provided us with a solid grounding in reading, writing and arithmetic, as well as some rudimentary knowledge of local history and geography. I still do all of my mental arithmetic in Hindi, using the multiplication tables drilled into us during those first four years in school.

When I entered grade five at the local middle school, which was funded by the State Government, I found that the facilities were much better. The classrooms were large, bright and airy, furnished with proper student desks and there was enough space for an office and common area for the teachers, as well for storing sports equipment. The school, which was a ten minute walk from our house, was built in 1905 and had extensive playgrounds with fields for soccer, field hockey, cricket and volleyball. It was at this little school in an obscure Indian town that I first learned the English alphabet and wrestled with the sometimes irrational pronunciation of English words – my mother-tongue, Hindi, is completely phonetic. By the end of grade eight, I was able to read and write in English, although my vocabulary was very limited and I lacked any conversational ability in the language. At the time, I had little inkling that this strange new language would open the doors to the world's largest knowledge base for me, and contribute so profoundly to my personal and professional development throughout my life.

A carefree boyhood

I grew up in a large extended family that spanned four generations. Our family life was mostly regulated by religious, community and caste traditions which provided a very stable and protective environment for a child like me to develop his physical and intellectual potential, surrounded by a strong sense of physical safety and unconditional love. The basic norms of behaviour and social conduct were inculcated from an early age, and any significant departures would be noticed and duly dealt with by a senior member of the family, or an elder from the neighbourhood or the community at large. Under the informal supervision of the adults around us, the children were free to indulge in their own pastimes, with little direction and interference from the adults.

My daily routine as a child was very simple: awake before sunrise, morning walk, a glass of milk for breakfast, play outside with friends until school time, bath followed by morning meal, attend school (10:00 am to 4:30 pm), return from school and play outside with friends until sunset, evening meal followed by a family gathering when an adult family member would tell or read stories, and finally to bed around 9:00 pm. I trace my life-long love of reading to these nightly sessions of storytelling and reading while sitting around a dim kerosene lamp and, in winter, around a wood-burning brazier. Since there were no libraries in the local schools or a public lending library in town, and few people subscribed to the handful of Hindi magazines which were published, we had to scrounge for old Hindi magazines and books or translations of Western books that happened to be around. It now feels strange that I first encountered authors like Conan Doyle, Chekhov, and du Maupassant during these nightly reading sessions as a young boy growing up in a little town in India. It is even stranger when I think about my visit to Portofino, near Genoa in Italy, more than 50 years later, sitting in a restaurant and being told that the house across the narrow channel was where du Maupassant had lived and written his delightful stories.

I do not think that I endured any major medical problems that would have caused my parents any serious concern. I suffered the usual seasonal ailments like malaria, and dysentery in the rainy season, severe colds in the winter, and heat strokes in the summer, as well as common childhood diseases like measles, mumps, and frequent ear and stomach aches. I along with most children in town, frequently had slivers or thorns in our feet, scraped toes, and cold sores around our heels. Footwear for young children was considered a luxury – I did not have a proper pair of shoes until I was thirteen years old and did not wear shoes on a regular basis until I left for the city for further education. We also went through a few cholera outbreaks, as well as a severe outbreak of bubonic plague that forced our family to flee the town and camp out in the surrounding woods for more than a month.

Life for me as a youngster was easy and uncomplicated and I had ample freedom to explore the town and its surrounding area on my own or with my friends. I had a lot of friends in our neighbourhood, as well as in other parts of town, and I grew up with a warm feeling of belonging in an expanding circle of family, neighbourhood and the town. Away from school, we had no supervised activities and we devised our own simple games and decided on our own recreational agendas. The games we played were determined by the season. In the monsoon season, it was mostly marbles; in the winter, some type of ball game with handmade balls and simple sticks. In the summer, it would be making and flying kites – and running after kites which lost in a kite fight, just as described in the best-selling book, The Kite Runner, by Khaled Hosseini. I spent many hot summer afternoons making kites, preparing a paste containing fine-ground glass, and rubbing it on lengths of thread for kite fights in the evening. Summer mornings were often spent at the local river, swimming to the far shore and exploring the terrain and picking wild berries. In the hot summer evenings, we frequently went down to the market square and gathered around the shaved-ice vendor to enjoy a cup of shaved ice with a choice of different flavours of sweet syrups. This was a special treat because ordinarily ice was a rare commodity in our town, and the vendor had to bring a block of ice, covered in sawdust to minimize melting, every day from the District town, 40 km away.

Soon after I entered middle school, a new family moved into our neighbourhood. The father was a primary school teacher and the family had a son my age who was enrolled in my class. We became good friends and the friendship continued for many years until I graduated from college and he moved away to work in a distant town. In addition to being a teacher, the father soon became well known as a handyman who could repair almost any mechanical gadget, including clocks, watches, gramophones and firearms. As a young boy, I found their house was like a Pandora's Box, with all kinds of fascinating tools and gadgets, and more importantly, a BB gun, as well as many indoor games, including chess, snakes and ladders and carom board. Growing up in a small town, listening to gramophone records, learning to play chess, and target shooting with the BB gun were rare and memorable experiences for me. On Sunday afternoons in good weather, my new friend and I, accompanied at times by a few other boys from the neighbourhood, would explore the woods north of the town. In addition to collecting wild berries and exploring the woods and the streams that cut across them, we would also shoot birds, such as partridges and wild doves, with the BB gun. My friend's family, who were not vegetarian, would then cook the bounty for their evening meal. I have to confess that I tasted a non-vegetarian dish for the first time when my friend invited me to join him to share the day's shoot at his house. However, my encounters with poultry, fish, and meat were few and far between until I went to live for extended periods of time in the West.

My first eight years at school were mostly carefree and happy, and generally protected from external events and upheavals, such as distant wars, the raging struggle for independence and devastating famines and suffering. Our teachers were experienced, competent, conscientious and well-respected not only by the students but also by the town's population at large. Living in a small town, there was little opportunity to play hooky, although when I was in my last year of middle school, I did manage to go on a couple of short trips without first telling my parents. The first time, I decided to accompany a friend on a Saturday to the District town to see a popular movie. We stayed overnight with his relatives, took in the matinee show, and returned home on Sunday evening. The second time, another friend talked me into spending *Diwali* in the city of Jabalpur at his married sister's house. Again, we saw a couple of movies, but this time I got terribly homesick after two nights – I especially missed my mother's holiday goodies. On the third morning I said goodbye to my friend and his sister, walked 4 km through the unfamiliar city to the bus station, and caught a bus home. In both instances, my parents quickly found out about where I had gone – the joys of living in a small town – and knew that I was safe and sound and would eventually be home. I do not recall my parents making a big fuss about my behaviour.

On the home front, I enjoyed all the advantages of living in an extended family which had a deep respect for learning and the acquisition of knowledge. The story telling and reading sessions that were part of our family tradition left a lasting impression on me. In the summers, our family was extended even more when my aunt, my father's older sister, and her children came for long visits. The concept of annual vacations and family holidays was unheard of when I was a child, and I did not come across this Western custom until I went to Canada many years later. The only time our family traveled any distance from home was either to visit distant family members for special occasions, such as a wedding, or an important festival or for a pilgrimage to one of the many temples and shrines which are in abundance all across India. The closest I came to rough outdoor living as a child was when I would accompany my grandmother on her yearly trip to oversee the harvesting on our lands, for a week or two in the early summer.

Our farming lands were located in another village about 4 km away from the town. The process used for harvesting the winter crops, which consisted of mostly wheat, garbanzo beans, and lentils, was very primitive and probably thousands of years old. The crops were cut by a team of itinerant hired labourers who used simple sickles, and the crop was then brought to a large circular harvesting compound. The compound was delineated by a fence made of branches from thorny bushes. A thick pole was erected in the middle of the compound, and a lean-to with a thatched roof in a corner of the compound served as our living quarters. To prevent the potential loss of the uninsured harvest by fire, the compound was built well away from the village, near a source of water, such as a well, and smoking or cooking in or near the compound was strictly forbidden. In order to separate the grain from the hay, loads of the freshly cut crops were spread around the central pole, and a team of bullocks, with mouth coverings, tethered to the pole, trampled the crop until the grains were separated from the husk. The next step in the process was to use wind power to separate the grain from the husk: specifically, a person would stand on a tall stool, slowly releasing the mixture into the strong afternoon breeze so that the heavier grain kernels collected close to the stool while the husk was blown some distance away. I greatly enjoyed this short break from my routine at home – especially the morning and evening picnics for which my grandmother cooked simple country meals, and the time I spent wandering around the nearby villages and farms in search of wild berries and fruits.

Another custom that was unfamiliar to me was the concept of celebrating birthdays and exchanging gifts. In fact, I did not discover the exact birthdates of my siblings or my parents until I applied for security clearance to do some consulting work for the Canadian Government and had to provide the information to the RCMP. I do not recall anyone in our family, our community, or our town having a birthday party. In fact, the first time anyone had a birthday party for me was when Margaret successfully arranged a surprise birthday party for my 31st birthday in 1963. It was a double surprise because she had the wrong date.

Festivals and fairs

One of the joys of growing up in a small town within a close-knit community was the enjoyment of numerous religious festivals and country fairs, or *Melas*, associated with some of these festivals that took place in and around the town. India is a country populated by people of many faiths, including Hindus,

Buddhists, Jains and Sikhs, who follow religions indigenous to India, as well as by Muslims, Christians, Zoroastrians, and Jews who brought their religions with them to India over a period of almost two millennia. As such the festivals in India not only celebrate important events from the rich history and mythology associated with Hinduism, but also celebrate key events from other religions practised in India. As a child, the festivals that I especially looked forward to included the Hindu festivals of *Navaratri* (nine nights) which precede the *Dussehra* festival; *Diwali,* the festival of lights that celebrates the victory of good over evil; *Holi*, the festival of colour to herald the spring harvest and the observance of *Muharram* or *Ashurah* which marks the martyrdom of Hussein ibn Ali, the grandson of Prophet Muhammad at the battle of Karbala in 680 CE.

Navaratri

While *Navaratri* is celebrated in many parts of India under differing tags (for example *Durga Pooja* in Bengal), it is the primary festival for Gujaratis and has a special significance for our family. During these nine days, our family deity is brought out from its private quarters in our temple and moved to a viewing area consisting of a specially built, covered patio where people would come for *Darshan*, or spiritual viewing. The area immediately around the display was decorated with specially built panels; inverted glass bells of various sizes and colours, in which candles could be lit, were hung from the ceiling, and framed pictures were displayed, depicting religious themes from Hindu mythology, including some reproductions of paintings by the famous Indian painter Ravi Varma. There was room in the front for the visiting devotees to sit and admire the tableau as well as room for the group of *garba* dancers to perform their vigorous dances, accompanied by loud clapping and devotional songs. The *garba* dance is a famous folk dance of Gujarat which is commonly performed during the *Navaratri* season, along with the *dandia* dance using sticks. It is one of the gifts that our expatriate community brought to the town and has now spread, as people from the community have moved throughout the region.

During the nine days of *Navaratri*, the display was changed every few days to show the deity in different poses representing mythological events associated with the Divine Mother. The most important of these was the display on the eighth day of *Navaratri*, called *Durga Ashtmi*, which depicted the goddess *Durga* with eight hands in a black *sari,* riding a tiger, with a *trishule* (three-pronged

71

Indian lance), in her hand, piercing the cowering body of the buffalo demon, *Mahishasura*. Since I was accustomed to seeing the deity in our temple in the form of a rigid clay sculpture of a short, standing female with four hands, as a small child, I was always intrigued and puzzled by the displays that showed her riding a tiger with eight hands or sitting on a lotus flower. Finally, the puzzle was solved when I began to accompany my father during the afternoons when he would change the display. I found that the illusion was accomplished with the help of appropriately shaped extra legs and hands made of *papier-mâché*. These were strategically placed and tied to the main sculpture, with the clothing and accessories arranged to help create the illusion.

It is also traditional during this period for many towns and cities to have performances of *Ram Lila,* a play that tells the story of *Ramayana,* one of the two major Hindu epics – the other being *Mahabharat,* the longest verse ever written. In our town, the *Ram Lila* was held in the small open market, with the stage set at one end and the audience sitting on shop fronts or the open space. The ten-day performance started every evening around 9:00 pm and continued until late at night with an all-male cast. Female roles were played by teenage boys, just as in Shakespeare's time.

On the home front, the *Navaratri* celebration involved its own set of activities and rituals – partly in support of the daily displays at the temple and partly to conform to long-established traditions. Every morning, I would go to the neighbouring houses which had flowering plants such as roses, jasmine and marigolds and collect a basketful of flowers. My sisters and I would then prepare garlands from these flowers for the evening display at the temple. Most of the adult females in the household and a few males would observe a fast during the nine days of *Navaratri* and would be restricted to having one special meal in the early afternoon. This meal generally consisted of fruits and specially prepared dishes made from ingredients such as *ghee* (clarified butter), sugar, sago, peanuts, and poppy seeds. The meal was consumed only after it was properly blessed by the family goddess. On *Dussehra,* the tenth day, pre-teen boys and girls from the community were invited for a mid-day feast and the meal was served on banana leaves which I had to fetch from a banana grove at a relative's house.

Diwali

The festival of *Diwali*, also known as festival of lights, which occurs about twenty days after *Dussehra*, is probably the best known of the Hindu festivals. It is a time for families to get together and for children and adults to indulge in public displays of joy and goodwill. It is also the day when people pay special homage to *Lakshmi*, the goddess of wealth and prosperity. In our home, after the *Lakshmi Pooja* the house was decorated inside and out with small earthen lamps filled with vegetable oil and each fashioned with a cotton wick. The children, who had been hoarding a variety of fireworks, would go out and start lighting them. Neighbourhood kids would come over, bringing their own goodies, and we would spend hours having a great deal of fun, with the adults joining in. One of the *Diwali* traditions is to indulge in gambling, generally using a simple card game called *teen patti* (three cards). It is similar to poker in its betting protocols but the game is so simple that a child can learn it in a few minutes. On *Diwali* night, many adults and children in town would get together in small groups for sessions of *teen patti* – of course, the level of bets would vary widely. I was inducted into the game at a tender age and continued to play it from time to time well into my adulthood in India.

Holi

The celebration of *Holi*, also called festival of colors has two distinct parts: first, the lighting of a large bonfire the night before the festival and then the throwing of coloured water and powder in which the whole town participates, regardless of caste, creed, or religion. My friends and I would start collecting wood for the bonfire well in advance by going door-to-door in the neighbourhood, stealing wood from residents who were not careful enough to store it safely, and stealthily cutting tree branches from the surrounding woods. We also collected small amounts of money from the households for our efforts to collect wood for the bonfire, and divided the money amongst ourselves to buy sweets.

Often in the afternoon when the color-throwing activities were over, my older brothers would prepare the special drink used traditionally in North India as a mix for marijuana, after the latter has been soaked and ground into a paste. Most members of the family, including women and children, were allowed to have the drink with moderate amounts of marijuana in it, which sometimes induced an unstoppable riot of laughter during the evening meal. This cooling drink and little balls of marijuana paste (sold separately) were commonly sold by street vendors in many North Indian cities during the summer months. This practice was especially popular in Varanasi, the city dedicated to Lord Shiva who supposedly favours this drink to cool his burning throat, the cause of which is part of the Hindu mythology. This is also the reason why most depictions show Lord Shiva with a cobra wrapped around his neck because the cobra's skin is supposed to be cold and soothing.

Muharram or Ashura

While Muharram or *Ashurah* is actually a commemoration of a historic event for Shia Muslims rather than a festival, the way it was observed in our town, as well as in towns and cities in North India, made for a great deal of fun for young children. The preparations began months in advance when a Muslim family in our neighbourhood would start to assemble a large *papier maché* float, called a *tazzia*, representing the bier of the martyrs. On the day of *Ashura*, which is the tenth day in the month of Muharram in the Islamic Lunar calendar, the *tazzias* built by different neighbourhoods would form a procession which I and my friends from the neighbourhood would join in shouting *ya Hussein, ya Ali*, in mourning for the martyrs. The ritual mourning for the martyrs takes different forms in different parts of the Islamic world, including self flogging, self stabbing, and breast beating. After winding through the town, the mourning procession of the tazzias would end up at the large open market where the *tazzias* would be lined up for the population to admire their beauty and workmanship. As the night fell, the marketplace would morph into a *mela* with vendors selling a variety of goods, mostly for children. One of our favourite items was a type of trail mix containing coconut flakes, raisins, cashews, almonds, sesame seeds, cardamom seeds, and sugar crystals.

Makar Sankranti

The Hindu festival of *Makar Sankranti* is celebrated across India, although under different names and somewhat different connotations. It is based on the solar calendar and always falls around January 14th, the day the sun starts its northward journey. All Hindus are supposed to have a ritual bath on this day, preferably by dipping into one of the seven holy rivers, the Ganges being one of them. In our house, the ritual bath had two stages. In the first stage, a paste made of a mixture of lentil flours, mustard oil, herbs, and water was applied to our bodies and, once it was properly set, was slowly rubbed off. The process resulted in a thorough cleaning of the skin and opening of the pores, similar to some of the procedures used in many Western spas today. The second stage involved a thorough soaking and scrubbing with almost scalding water. However, for me as a child, this festival was special because it was the day of the largest *mela* in our region, which was held on the banks of the river about 10 km downstream from our town. It was a long distance to walk there and back for a child. Fortunately, our Muslim neighbours (children and ladies) always drove to the site in their bullock cart and I was always welcome to join the party. My parents gave me some spending money and we would leave after the morning meal and would not return until after sunset, excited, exhausted, and full of sweets and candy floss.

Gypsies and pilgrims

In addition to the various festivals and fairs during the year, we also looked forward to the annual arrival of the gypsies and other travellers who passed through our town, making temporary camp for a few days before moving on to their next destination. Their arrival was sudden and unannounced. One morning we would find a group of 20 or 25 strangely and colourfully dressed people setting up their camp under a large shady tree not far from our house. They would have three or four brightly painted bullock carts of a design not seen in our region which carried all their worldly belongings, as well as the children who were too small to walk.

This group of gypsies earned their living as ironmongers, and they made or repaired such items as rims for bullock cart wheels, implements used by farmers, and household tools, such as knives and axes. The gypsy women were always dressed in very colourful, long, flared skirts, with skimpy blouses tied at the back and they had their hands covered from wrist to elbow in multi-coloured bangles. They were hardy women and we watched in awe as a pair of them, standing opposite each other, would work heavy sledge hammers in perfect rhythm to pound a piece of red hot iron, which one of the male members manipulated on the anvil into the desired shape. At times, I was afraid that if one of the women lost her grip, the hammer would fly straight at the other woman and kill her, but it of course, never happened.

The gypsies had their own language, which, I believe, was a dialect of a language from Western India, and they usually kept to themselves and were rarely seen in the town proper. Their children roamed the surrounding fields to catch wild creatures, such as snakes and squirrels, which we were told the gypsies considered as delicacies. Another group of gypsies that passed through our town came with herds of cattle, many of which carried sacks filled with a type of material mined in Western India which is used to prepare the whitewashing solution for houses. These gypsies arrived before the festival of *Diwali* when most households whitewash their houses after the monsoon rains to make them clean and shiny for the festival. Some times I wonder if it was the forefathers of these gypsies from Western India who decided to travel West instead of East and ended up in Europe a long time ago, and their descendents are now referred as Roma in Europe - an alien group generally distrusted and maligned by the local population and marginalized by the authorities in many European countries.

The neo-gypsies were groups of pilgrims who became gypsies for four to six months while they walked to visit the holy places scattered all over India. These groups of pilgrims would temporarily camp on the outskirts of town as they proceeded on their journey. All their daily needs were contained in a couple of wicker baskets hung at the two ends of a bamboo pole which they carried on their shoulders. It was very pleasant to hear the pilgrims sing their melodious, religious songs as they camped or walked on their journey.

Events in India and abroad

When I was in middle school, World War II was underway, although initially its impact on our lives in Hatta was minimal. There were no radios in town and only a handful of people subscribed to newspapers, so information about the war was scant. However, in the later stages of the war, acute shortages of salt, sugar and other food staples, as well as other goods, such as gasoline and kerosene oil, became widespread. The scarcity of gasoline resulted in drastic reductions in the bus service in and out of town, and the few buses that served the town were converted to run on what was called 'coal gas'. Although there were no severe food shortages in our region, the 1943 famine in Bengal took a heavy toll, with almost three million people loosing their lives. In spite of pleas from the Indian national leaders, the British government was either too busy defending its island nation from the Germans or too indifferent to the plight of their colonial subjects, to make meaningful efforts to avert the tragedy – a tragedy some times referred as the forgotten and avoidable holocaust. It is also believed that Prime Minister Churchill's antipathy towards India and its people may also have contributed to the British administrations' tardy response to the developing tragedy.

This was also the period when Mahatma Gandhi launched the 'Quit India' movement, a nationwide civil disobedience campaign to gain full independence from the British rule. Acting on the call by Gandhi, thousands of people from all over India, from all walks of life, including all the leaders of the national movement, defied the British Raj and they were incarcerated. My oldest brother was greatly influenced by Gandhi's ideas of civil disobedience and when the Quit India movement started he was at home and started his own clandestine campaign of writing and distributing pamphlets against the British rule. Our house was raided and searched by the police for incendiary material and proof of his anti-government activities. Somehow, my father was able to persuade the magistrate to spare my brother from being put in jail. However, in hindsight, it might have been better if he had spent a year or two as a political prisoner because, after India became independent in a few years the new government initiated an affirmative action scheme for so called 'freedom fighters' and their families who had suffered hardships at the hands of the British administration.

A tragedy in the family

It was around this time that my older sister became a widow. She was in her early twenties, mother of a two year old daughter and expecting another child in a few months. This was also the period when our family was in some what of an unsettled frame of mind owing to a number of anxiety-inducing factors including the near incarceration of my older brother for his activities in support of Gandhi's Quit India movement. My father was suffering from acute sciatic pain and was confined to his bed until my aunt (his older sister) insisted that he accompany her to Jhansi (her hometown) where he would receive much better medical attention. His absence from home was rarest of a rare event and it disturbed the normal rhythm of our household. My brother-in-law who was also a follower of Gandhi and used to work at Gandhi's Ashram at a place called

Wardha, had unfortunately contracted an intestinal disease resulting in acute diarrhea and dehydration. He was receiving medical attention – also in Jhansi his hometown, where his old father (a widower) now lived. My sister was currently at our home because traditionally in our community girls went home to their parents for the delivery of their first two or three children. Besides these internal family matters, the effects of WWII were starting to filter down to our remote town, resulting in frequent shortages of essential and not so essential goods, thus further exacerbating the unsettled atmosphere in the household.

One late afternoon I came home from school, dropped my book bag and was ready to step out again to play with my friends when the postman brought the afternoon mail with a letter from my father. My elder brother, who was barely twenty years old at the time, was nominal head of the household while my father was away. He started reading the letter and I could feel that it had brought some sad news because his eyes were starting to tear up. The family, including my sister, was already gathered around him and he disclosed the contents of the letter which included the news that my sister's husband had passed away and the letter also contained my father's instructions on the rituals which should be followed with regard to my sister becoming a widow. On hearing the news my sister holding on to her two year old daughter, started crying, my mother started wailing and my grandmother started praying and invoking our family deity's help to get us through this family tragedy. I and my young siblings stood around them, rather subdued and confused because we could not fully appreciate the tragic consequences of our sister becoming a widow at such a young age.

Up until recently, in most Hindu communities remarriage for a widow was not an option and especially for young widows it meant an uncertain future. In many cases the young widow was considered a burden and neglected and ill-treated by her husband's family which often blamed her for bringing bad luck to the family. Her parents on the other hand, were often reluctant to welcome her back either because they lacked the financial resources to support her and her children for an extended period or they felt that having given her away in marriage (often with a hefty dowry) they had done their duty by her and had no further obligations for her upkeep. Deepa Mehta's well known movie *WATER* highlights the plight of young Hindu widows in early twentieth century who were abandoned by their families, deserted by the society and left to fend for them selves with little support. Given the time and prevailing circumstances, my sister was headed for a rough ride unless our family lined up solidly by her side to provide material and emotional support in the dark days ahead. With one stroke of misfortune she was being deprived of the pleasures and privileges of a married woman and facing a life without a loving husband who could wipe her tears and comfort her when she was in pain and rejoice with her on their children's achievements – large and small.

Normally in our community when a woman became a widow she would be taken to the banks of the local river accompanied by the older women of the household and a barber. All the symbols of her being a married woman would be removed – especially the *mangal sutra* (auspicious necklace), the red mark on her forehead and all her jewelry. Her long hair would be shorn to the scalp by the barber and she would change into a simple white sari after a bath in the river. In other words she would be made as unattractive as possible as a woman and would remain so for the rest of her life. However, according to my father's instructions, my sister was taken to a nearby body of water (a man made pond) by our mother and grandmother where she went through the ritual except that her long hair remained intact – a pioneering and trend-setting departure from the established norms. There was no question of my sister returning to her in-laws house firstly because my father had already decided that she and her children would stay as an integral part of our family, and secondly because her husband's family did not have the financial resources to support her for the rest of her life.

After his return from Jhansi my father started planning to ensure that our widowed sister would become self supporting and financially independent. Within a year and after her second daughter was born, he hired a tutor for her so that she could upgrade her educational qualifications in order to qualify for entry to the teachers training school. Within a few years she completed the teachers training course and started teaching at the local public school for girls, and remained in the profession until she retired. My father also built her a small house next door to ensure that she and her children would always have a place of their own. However, most of the time she and her children lived with us as part of our extended family. Unfortunately, a few years after losing her husband she lost her older daughter as well, who accidentally drowned in the local river – another tragedy in her life that she certainly did not need.

Hinduism: part of everyday life

I was born into a Hindu, Brahmin family belonging to a small expatriate community with its origins in Gujarat in Western India. Each of these individual associations implies certain commitments and obligations. For example, as a member of a small expatriate community, I was obliged to preserve the traditional social customs of my forefathers, and as a member of the Brahmin priestly class, it was expected that I would embrace learning and the acquisition of knowledge as my primary obligation. However, since Hinduism is very non-doctrinaire in its approach, with a very distributed regulatory structure that allows, and even encourages individual interpretations of its extensive religious texts, it is almost impossible to define a set of clear obligations for a Hindu.

There is nothing in Hinduism comparable to the Ten Commandments or the defined duties of a practising Muslim, such as praying five times a day facing towards Mecca, fasting during Ramadan or going to Hajj. There is nothing in Hinduism like the principles of the *middle path* for a Buddhist, or the duties of a baptised Sikh prescribed in Guru Granth Sahib, the holy book of Sikhism. In Hinduism, there are no obligations to go to a specific place of worship on a specified day and there are no entities similar to a priest, minister, Rabbi, or an Imam who influence their flocks and look after their spiritual needs on a regular basis in a structured environment. Similarly, there are no equivalents to Sunday school, Yeshivas, or Madarssas to formally impart lessons on our religion or mythology or to instruct on issues of morality and ethics.

As a child, my induction into and knowledge of Hinduism and its extensive mythology and highly varied practices came about mainly by observing my family's religious and spiritual practices, and was supplemented by listening to and reading stories from the *Mahabharat,* the *Ramayan* and other religious texts, attending religious plays, and attending discourses from itinerant holy men who happened to be passing through town. In Hatta, symbols of Hindu faith were in abundance in the form of large temples and small shrines, which in many cases were simply a small statue or a simple *Shiva Lingam* under a Peepal or Banyan tree. As children, we visited these temples at our pleasure, viewing them more as places to gather and play rather than places to further our spiritual consciousness.

Our favourite temple was located less than 200 meters from our home and was dedicated to the goddess *Chandi,* another manifestation of the Divine Mother, more commonly called goddess *Kali.* The temple was a large and spacious complex consisting of a number of other shrines dedicated to various deities, a set of rooms where travellers could stay overnight, a stepped well for drinking water, i.e., a well with built-in steps to reach the water level, a large man-made pond which filled up to the brim in the monsoon and was popular for swimming. There was also a special room facing the temple where a ritual called *Hawan,* was occasionally conducted, usually funded by a devotee to thank the goddess *Chandi* for fulfilling a wish, such as the birth of a son. In this round-the-clock ritual, a number of priests would sit around the sacred fire, recite ancient Sanskrit hymns in praise of *Chandi* and make offerings of clarified butter, rice and herbs to the sacred fire at the end of each verse.

Moral values and ethical behaviour were essentially the products of the carrot and stick approach adopted by the extended family and to some extent by our teachers who praised us for acting in a certain manner or punished us when we did not. I remember one of my middle school teachers always quoting the phrase, 'if wealth is lost nothing is lost, and if health is lost some thing is lost, but if character is lost every thing is lost'. Unfortunately, he never elaborated on what he meant by character and left us with the impression that *character* was only concerned with sexual behaviour, i.e., the pursuit of the opposite sex, homosexuality and masturbation, and had little to do with honesty, generosity, courage, or ethical behaviour in general.

An event that occurred when I was in grade seven was especially significant towards my moral education. One afternoon after the end of classes at school, I was walking home along my normal route which went past the bungalow of the tahsildar, the highest administrative officer in town. About half way along my journey, I found a bill for one hundred rupees – an amount equivalent to more than three months' salary for a teacher. When I got home, I showed the bill to my older sister and told her where I found it. She immediately confiscated it and told my mother who told my father when he returned from his day's business. By the next morning, the lost one hundred rupee bill was a hot topic in the bazaar, and it was easy for my father to find out who had lost it. The poor man was an account clerk in a shop that we patronized and the amount probably represented a very large sum for him. It seems he was going for a business visit to the tahsildar and the bill, which was tucked into his *dhoti,* had somehow slipped out. My father went to the tahsildar that afternoon and told him how I had found the bill. The bill was returned to the owner who awarded me ten rupees as a prize for being honest and the school held a special award ceremony during the morning assembly to reinforce the value of honesty.

During my early years at our ancestral home, religion was part of everyday life. Hindu beliefs and practices were woven into our daily routine, and most activities reflected some aspect of the Hindu faith. In addition to religious festivals and associated activities, there were many other Hindu holy days in the year that led to fasting and/or special offerings to some god or goddess. Priests were constantly visiting the house to perform special *pooja* – for events such as births, deaths and weddings, and to conduct thread ceremonies which were obligatory for Brahmin boys and the annual *Shradha* ceremony to honour the ancestors. My early years at home within my extended family and close-knit community are primarily responsible for my knowledge of Hindu mythology and the underlying principles of the Hindu view of life, as well as for whatever moral and ethical values I have retained in my adult life.

After I left home, these close encounters with Hindu traditions and practices progressively declined to the extent that years later, even while living in India, my exposure to religious practice was mostly on a superficial level. I continue to call myself a Hindu because I was born into the faith, but not because I actively pursue its traditional practices. In the Hindu tradition, one may worship God through three paths which consist of: Knowledge, Action and Devotion, and a Hindu can choose one or more of these depending on his/her inclination and ability for abstract thought. On my journey through life I have veered away from one or more of these paths. However, in spite of the layers of rationality and cynicism that have overshadowed my childhood experience, the religious roots planted in those early years are still alive, if barely, because in moments of distress and despair I still visualize our little family goddess benevolently dispensing blessings to all her devotees – past and present.

CHAPTER 4

From a small town to a small city

In the spring of 1946, four months before my fourteenth birthday I graduated from grade eight near the top of my class and was ready to enrol in a high school for the next phase of my education. Since there were no higher educational facilities in Hatta, I knew that I would have to go to a larger town and that my days at home with my extended family were numbered. At this stage I did not have the faintest idea where I would go, because my parents – actually, my father – had not yet decided on a specific option. The choices were limited: either I would be sent off to a distant place with suitable educational facilities to live with a relative, or I would have to live in a residence in the nearest town with a high school, which happened to be Damoh, the district town, two hours away by bus. My two oldest brothers had lived with my aunt at Jhansi while attending high school and my third brother was billeted in a residence while attending high school at Damoh. My father was in a bit of a quandary because he did not want to impose further on his sister, but he felt that without proper supervision my third brother had slacked off while living unsupervised at a residence which resulted in unsatisfactory grades at his high school graduation.

Fortunately, towards the end of the summer when things were getting a bit desperate, a solution materialized. My uncle, who was visiting us, offered to have me live with him and attend high school in Raipur, a small city with a population of about 300,000, about 400 km southeast of our home. My uncle was the youngest of my father's siblings and was much younger, closer to my oldest sister's age. My grandfather had passed away when my uncle was still a child, and my father essentially raised him as one of his own children. At this time, my uncle was in his early twenties, a bachelor working as a stenographer in one of the temporary army establishments which proliferated during WWII.

It was decided that my grandmother would accompany us to set up a proper household for my uncle and me And thus my future, at least for the next few years, was settled, and I looked forward with great excitement to moving from a small town to a city with many movie houses, shops, and new sights and sounds to explore

On a cloudy morning in late June, after the monsoon season had arrived, I embarked on my journey to pursue the next phase of my education, accompanied by my uncle and grandmother. I packed my meagre belongings, mostly clothes, in a small tin suitcase and tied my bedding into a roll. My mother prepared a stack of *parathas* (Indian fried bread), along with potato *subji* and mango pickles and some sweets for our long journey. With a couple of hired neighbourhood women carrying our baggage on their heads, we left on foot for the bus station where we boarded the bus for the two-hour trip to the nearest railway station in the district town of Damoh.

Our journey did not start on an auspicious note. When we reached the railway station in Damoh, we discovered that the train that was supposed to carry us to our next connecting train had been cancelled and there was no other train available until the next day. Although the war had ended in Europe and Japan, transport facilities were still being deployed for the demobilization of British Indian troops and frequent delays and cancellations of civilian transport were common. We spent the night at a *Dharamsala*, a charity-funded inn for travelers, near the railway station, and finally caught the train for the first of the three legs of our train journey. As luck would have it, the train for the second leg had also been cancelled until a bridge on the track, which had been damaged by heavy monsoon rains, could be repaired. We spent that night sleeping on the floor of the station waiting room and were finally able to board the train late the next day. Fortunately, the last leg of our train journey went relatively smoothly and we arrived at the Raipur station after spending more than 72 hours on the journey. We took a *Tonga* (horse drawn carriage) to my uncle's apartment, which was located close to the city centre.

The city and the region

Raipur is the largest city in a region called *Chhattisgarh* (thirty-six forts) which was part of the Central Provinces and Berar, a province within British India for administrative purposes. The local Hindi dialect spoken in the region is called *Chhattigarhi* and is quite different from the dialect spoken in my hometown. The landscape is much flatter than that of our home region, with fields covered in rice plants. Rice is the main component in the regional cuisine, rather than wheat, as in our home region. As the name implies, before Indian independence, there were a large number of princely states in the region ruled by Rajas. Raipur was famous for the Rajkumar College (College for Princes) which was an exclusive private school where the male children of the Princely rulers in the region were educated. The College was located on an impressive and spacious campus, with buildings that could be compared to some of the prestigious British 'public' schools. After Independence, all the princely states were abolished and the college became a private school open to anyone who could afford it. The region is also very rich in natural resources, such as iron and coal. These natural resources in the region were increasingly harnessed after India gained independence and have led to the construction of the Bhilai Steel Plant, one of the largest in the country, as well as the expansion of transport infrastructure for exporting coal from the region to Japan and other South-East Asian countries.

Besides being the main civil administration hub for the region, Raipur is also an important rail transport hub with direct links to Bombay and Calcutta, as well as to the port city of Vishakpatnam on the Bay of Bengal and other important regional towns. Most businesses, shops, and markets in the city were clustered along the thoroughfare called Bensley Road now called Mahatma Gandhi Road or simply MG Road. Bensley Road was book-ended by the city *Kotwali*, the main police station, at the south end and the Imperial Bank on the north, with the main post and telegraph office and municipal buildings in between. The eastern part of the city was much more open because it housed most of the government administrative facilities, such as the district administrative offices, the district jail, the district hospital, the city park, the senior civil servants' club and their spacious residences. The railway station and its administrative offices and employee residences, occupied the northwest corner of the city, along with the usual commercial establishments, such as cheap hotels, restaurants, tea and paan shops, that seem to spring up around Indian railway stations. Aesthetically, the city had little to offer and there were no nearby attractions to qualify it as a tourist destination. There were no major industries in town at the time and the only two major employers were the government (local, provincial and federal) and the railways, which were privately owned before India gained independence. During the war, a couple of organizations related to the war effort were located around the city, but these were wound up after the war making most of the employees redundant. My uncle was one of the casualties, having worked at the

Army Medical Store which acted as the clearing house for basic medical and surgical supplies for the British Indian Army units in the country.

When I arrived in Raipur, the city's educational, medical and entertainment facilities consisted of: four high schools, a private humanities college that was run on a shoestring budget and was housed in a crumbling old bungalow; a small government-run hospital with the only qualified general surgeon in the area and about half-a-dozen qualified physicians and three movie houses that showed only Bollywood movies. It was a typical small city, with no special features to distinguish it from any other similar-sized city in India. However, as our *Tonga* made its way through various neighbourhoods to my uncle's apartment, to a young boy coming from a small town, the sights and sounds of the city generated a level of anticipation and excitement that I have experienced only a few times since.

The neighbourhood

My uncle's apartment was located on a narrow street that was a ten-minute walk to Bensley Road, the city's main street. It consisted of three rooms on the second floor of a house and the front and back rooms were actually covered porches or balconies. One entered the apartment through the back room that looked out on the landlord's front courtyard and the back of a temple around the corner. The kitchen was a corner of the back room, with the rest of the space used as dining and living areas. The middle room was used for storage and sleeping. The front room looked out on the narrow street and was my favourite place for watching the on-going activities on the street. There was a small water-storage and bathing area in the front room which provided minimal privacy. We had to share a lavatory with the landlord's family who occupied the entire ground floor. There was no electricity or running water in the house and water for daily use had to be brought from the neighbourhood public water tap by a servant.

This was a mixed, lower middle class neighbourhood with most bread earners involved in some trade or small business. The area was called *Telipara*, neighbourhood of the oil merchants, because many of the families who lived there belonged to a caste that traditionally dealt in the production and sale of vegetable oils. However, very few of these families were actually in the oil business and generally earned their living by other means. For example, our landlord, although belonging to this caste, had a couple of franchises from the

State Government to operate country liquor outlets in the surrounding small towns. The only family that was actively engaged in the oil business was the Muslim family next door which operated a traditional oil press powered by bullocks. The press was modelled after a mortar and pestle: the bullocks were harnessed to the pestle and made to operate it in a circular motion, thereby squeezing the oil from the seeds in the mortar.

The only neighbourhood person we interacted with regularly was an old South Indian lady who lived alone a few houses down. An avid reader, she read Hindi books and magazines until well after midnight and never started her day before noon. She was always scrounging for reading material, and we soon started sharing whatever books and magazines we could lay our hands on. She was a very fussy and cantankerous old lady who was always at loggerheads with her next door neighbour about their noisy children. We never found out where this lady had come from, how she ended up in this city and this neighbourhood far away from her home, or how she supported herself financially.

Starting high school

The first priority on our arrival was to set up proper cooking facilities and fetch the necessary provisions and paraphernalia for a functioning household. My uncle, as a bachelor was not into cooking and had arranged to have two meals a day at a nearby establishment for a fixed monthly charge. His cooking at home was restricted to heating milk and making morning tea on a primus stove. The second urgent task was to find a place for me at a decent high school because the new school year was to commence shortly and most schools had already filled their admission quotas.

Fortunately, through an acquaintance my uncle learned that St. Paul High School, one of the better schools in the city, had decided at the last minute to expand their intake and I was accepted as a new student there. The school was funded and operated by a Methodist missionary organization based in the United States. Since the *Chhattisgarh* region has a large population of aboriginal people usually called *adivasis* in India, Christian Missionaries found it a fertile ground for their efforts to spread the Gospel. The missionaries also ran a number of other public institutions in the city, including a reading room, a recreational club, and a residence for Christian students and a facility for treating leprosy and other communicable diseases. St. Paul High School was located in a neighbourhood called Byron Bazaar on the outskirts of the city, about a half-hour walk from our house. It was a fairly large complex, with a number of buildings for classrooms, lecture theatres, science laboratories, a student residence, the Headmaster's residence, the student assembly hall and spacious grounds for sports.

On my first day at the new school, one of my uncle's friends gave me a ride in the rear carrier of his bicycle, because my uncle had to be at work and could not accompany me. That evening, I was able to find my way back home through the unfamiliar streets, but the next morning when I set out to walk to the school, I took a wrong turn and got lost. However, my generally good sense of direction came to the rescue, and I was able to find my way again without being late. I had opted for the science stream and was enrolled in what was called the 'English medium' meaning that all academic activity, except for Hindi literature, was carried out in English. In effect, I had entered the 'English immersion' stream, although it was a long time before I could carry on a conversation in English.

Exploring the new landscape

It did not take long for me to become familiar with the general layout of the city and feel confident finding my way around. I started taking different routes to and from the school so that I could explore various neighbourhoods in the city. I especially liked to walk through *Halwai Lane*, street of sweet makers and vendors, enjoying the tempting aromas and displays of fresh Indian sweets. I also enjoyed walking along the main street, Bensley Road, where some snake oil seller would often have his wares spread out near an intersection and would be giving his spiel to the crowd gathered around him. He would always start with a few slight-of-hand card tricks to attract and engage the crowd. Next, he would play on the sexual insecurity of young and middle-aged men by talking about the ill effects of masturbation on their sexual performance, finally finishing with the benefits of his products for enhancing sexual prowess and the promise of a blissful married life. More often than not, his spiel produced good results and he made quite a few sales. At my age, I was more interested in the slight-of-hand card tricks whose secrets he generally disclosed to the amazement and entertainment of the crowd.

My class had about twenty-five students, consisting of five girls and the rest boys. One of the girls lived on a farm some distance from the city and commuted to the school on a bullock cart. The girls always occupied the front row seats and there was no contact, verbal or otherwise, between the sexes. Although all the schools and universities I attended had co-educational classes, this unwritten protocol was seldom violated throughout my life as a student in India. This picture has changed dramatically over the last half century, however, and the sexes are mingling much more freely now, at least in the urban and semi-urban areas all over India, and can make life decisions that are not always constrained by old prejudices and traditions. I developed a crush on a Bengali girl who was in my class, not only in high school but also during my undergraduate years. It seems she moved to Calcutta and, as chance would have it, I also went there for post graduate studies but I never saw her again. Needless to say, I never had the occasion or courage to speak to her and I sometimes wonder how her life played out after her move to the big city.

My first four months in the city were filled with excitement and new experiences and passed quickly. It was not long before I started to look forward to the *Diwali* holidays in October, an opportunity to return home and see my parents, siblings, and old friends. However, I had just turned fourteen and my uncle was reluctant to let me embark on the long journey with multiple changes of trains and buses on my own. Fortunately, one of his acquaintances was travelling part of the way on the same route and agreed to look after me. I was able to make the rest of the journey on my own, carrying loads of fireworks and special sweets for *Diwali* celebrations. At the end of the holidays, I was able to make the return journey on my own without any major mishaps, and from then on was considered to be mature enough to travel alone on all manner of journeys.

On my next long journey I ran into difficulties probably caused by the character trait generally associated with the males of our species – reluctance to ask for directions. I had decided to spend part of my summer vacation with my cousins at my mother's home town of Shrikakulum in Southern India, about 300 km southeast from Raipur. The railway station nearest to the town is on the main track between Calcutta and Madras. The train from Raipur meets this track at a place called Vijaynagaram where I needed to change trains. My train from Raipur was a bit late arriving at this station, and when I saw another train on the opposite track, I assumed it was the train for my destination and boarded it. Soon after the train left the platform, I realized my mistake – in fact, it was headed back in the direction I had just come from. I was in a bit of a panic, mainly because I was in a region where people spoke a language that was essentially Greek to me. As a result, I made my maiden attempt to carry on a conversation in English, as I approached a co-traveller familiar with the region. He advised me to get off at a particular station and go to the local bus station where I would be able to catch a bus to my intended destination. I finally got off the bus at my final destination, and remembering the town's layout from my last visit at the age of five, made my way to my maternal uncle's home in the late evening, tired, hungry and in need of a bath.

A brief encounter with the RSS

Towards the end of my first year in high school, I got drawn into a youth organization called Rashtriya Swayamsevak Sangh (National Volunteer Organization), or simply RSS. I did not realize until later that this was a Hindu fundamentalist organization that recruited young boys to brainwash them, by preaching the superiority of Hindus and Hinduism over all other people and faiths in India. RSS was started in 1925 by Dr. Hedgewar, a Maharashtrian gentleman, in the Central Indian city of Nagpur. It is quite possible that Dr. Hedgewar's movement was motivated by the sense of lost glory when the Hindu Maratha dynasties that had ruled most of Western and Central India after the decline of the *Mugal* Empire were annexed by the British in the nineteenth century. Chhatrapati Shivaji, who waged a sustained guerrilla war against the *Mugals* and spearheaded the rise of these Maratha dynasties, continues to be venerated by the members and fellow travellers of RSS

At the time that I joined, RSS would establish *Shakhas* (classes) in urban and semi-urban locations where the young 'volunteers' would assemble every evening for drills, martial arts training and brief lectures by the class teacher, an adult senior RSS operative or an invited guest. Every evening I would go to the *Shakha* nearest my home, carrying a long bamboo staff, as a weapon for martial arts, dressed in the white shirt and khaki shorts of special design that identified RSS volunteers. RSS had its own small library in the city containing books about the somewhat revisionist history of Hindus in India, their heroes and their accomplishments. I remember reading a book from that library called *Ushaakaal* (The Dawn), a novel describing the exploits of Shivaji as a guerrilla warrior. Thankfully, my association with the RSS did not last very long. Within a year, my interests had shifted to reading, watching action movies and playing table tennis and volley ball. This was probably an early indication of what developed into a lifelong aversion to joining and being active in any type of group, club, or association – social, political, or religious.

Exploring English fiction

At the time I started living with my uncle, he and two of his friends subscribed to a number of Indian monthly magazines which they rotated among themselves. Two were Hindi magazines which carried mostly romantic short stories of low to medium quality, including columns for the lovelorn. They also subscribed to an English magazine simply called My Magazine which was rather thin and was printed on the cheapest available paper. It contained a few short stories, many crossword puzzles and a lot of advertisements, mostly of a dubious nature. However, in that English magazine I came across a series of stories called Swami and Friends by the famous Indian author R.K. Narayan. I was completely enchanted by these stories which described the adventures of a young boy called Swami growing up in a small South Indian town called Malgudi on the banks of a river – an Indian equivalent to Mark Twain's narratives about the adventures of Tom Sawyer and Huckleberry Finn. Perhaps the stories by R.K. Narayan resonated with me because they reminded me of my own experiences growing up in a town of similar size and ambience on the banks of a river. This series of stories about Swami and his friends was my first introduction to un-translated English fiction, and they motivated me to become more proficient in reading English and to explore a wider range of English reading material. Our high school English course included a book containing a wide range of short stories and essays. The two that left a lingering impression on me were the short story,' How Much Land Does a Man Need' by Leo Tolstoy, and the humorous essay 'The Indian Crow' by Mark Twain. I soon became a member of the Gauss Memorial Club and Library, operated by the Methodist Mission which provided a wider range of reading material as well as an opportunity to improve my table tennis game.

My initial interest in English fiction was slanted towards detective stories and I spent most of my pocket money at the A.H.Wheeler bookstall at the railway station, buying cheap paperback novels about the exploits of Sexton Blake, a private detective living on Baker Street in London, and his sidekick, Tinker. To my surprise, I later discovered that Sexton Blake is one of the most written about characters in the English language, representing a publishing phenomenon of the 20th century England with close to 5,000 Blake stories written by 200 authors – it seems I was in good company after all. By the time I left Raipur on completion of my undergraduate degree in 1953, my experience of English language writers had significantly widened to include such authors as Arthur Conan Doyle, Agatha Christie, Jane Austen, Oscar Wilde, Charles Dickens, P.G. Woodhouse, Mark Twain, as well as French authors, Alexander Dumas and Emile Zola. However, to this day, my interest in mystery novels and detective stories, especially by British authors, has never waned.

A taste for Bollywood action movies

The small town where I spent my early years had no movie house and the nearest town where we could see a movie was 40 km away, whereas Raipur had three movie houses, which had increased to six by the time I left. The closest we came to movies in my hometown were the 'magic lantern' shows that visiting Christian missionaries occasionally arranged for school children. These were essentially slide shows put on with a slide projecting contraption using a petromax, a pressurized kerosene lantern using a filament for a brighter light source, and a white-washed wall for a screen.

I saw my first movie when I was five years old while visiting my maternal uncle in South India. I must have tagged along with my cousins to the local movie shed where we all sat on the dirt floor and watched a local language movie called 'The Golden Horse'. Later, I saw some religious movies based on stories from the Hindu epics *Ramayana* and *Mahabharata* for which we had to travel to cities neighbouring our town. Coming from such a background, I was naturally attracted to movie shows and popular movie songs. Initially, when I started living with my uncle and he went to see a movie he would also take me along. At the time, Bollywood films could be classified into three basic categories: romantic, action and religious movies. My uncle preferred the romantic movies while I was more attracted to action movies, and so after some time we parted ways and I started watching action movies on my own.

At the time, some of the most popular Bollywood action films, generally called stunt movies, were *Hunterwali* (lady with the whip), *Hunterwali ki Beti* (Hunterwali's daughter), and *Toofan Queen* (Hurricane Queen), starring a young woman whose stage name was Nadia, as the fearless heroine, dressed in tight, revealing clothes, high boots, and an Australian bush hat. She was a very popular stunt actress, who performed her own stunts, and it was exciting to watch her fight with the villain on top of a moving train, which was fast approaching a narrow tunnel – with the whole movie house loudly egging her on. In many films, she performed provocative dance numbers in revealing outfits, further increasing her popularity among mostly Indian male audiences. Much later, I learned that Nadia's real name was Mary Ann Evans and she was born in Perth, Australia to a Scottish father and a Greek mother. She came to India at the age of five where her father was serving in the British Indian army. She was a good horseback rider and ballet dancer and she learned to perform stunts while working in a circus. The famous Bollywood producer of stunt films, J.B.H.Wadia, introduced her to Hindi action movies in 1933. His brother, Homi Wadia fell in love with Nadia but they could not get married until after his mother passed away because she was opposed to their inter-faith and inte-racial marriage. Nadia was fluent in Hindi and remained on the Bollywood movie scene from 1933 to 1970. She died in 1996, at the age of eighty-eight.

I was soon introduced to English films when one of the movie theatres started showing them as weekend matinees. The majority of these were either action movies, mostly cowboy Westerns, or comedies, both of which required only a minimal familiarity with the English language in order to enjoy them. It was great fun to watch Abbot & Costello, Laurel & Hardy, and Hope & Crosby do their comedy routines. During this period, I also saw a few mainstream films including: Casablanca, and was convinced that Ingrid Bergman was the most beautiful woman I had ever seen. Another movie I remember from this period was about a ballet dancer. It featured a lot of ballet performances whose artistic aspects I was too young to appreciate, although I was turned on by the young dancers whose tutus exposed their underwear and the outlines of their neat little butts. All in all, these English language movies provided me with a glimpse into the ways of the West and added more than a few new words to my English vocabulary.

Independence for India

While I was busy pursuing my high school studies and enjoying my time with friends and family, 1946 to 1949 was a critical period for the future of the Indian subcontinent. Britain had won the war, but in the process, had lost the taste for the Empire. Britain had lost the military and economic power, as well as the will to continue ruling India, even though it was considered the 'Jewel' in the British Crown'. Britain was looking for a speedy exit from India so that it could focus on putting its own economic and social house in order. Their undue haste to hand over power, the understandable impatience of the Indian leaders to get rid of the colonizers, and the polarization between communities created by the 'divide and rule' policies of the British Raj made for a toxic situation. This resulted in the partition of India which was undertaken with little thought or planning to prevent the horrific consequences that soon unfolded. Almost a million innocent people were slaughtered on both sides of the divide, and millions more were displaced and suffered untold misery and trauma resulting in the largest migration of people in recorded history. This unprecedented tragedy seems to have permanently affected the psyche of the population and, 60 years after the events, the repercussions are still being felt. The British colonial practice of drawing national boundaries based on politics or expediency has led to unending conflicts and unnecessary loss of life and property in Africa, the Middle East and Asia. Since Raipur was far away from the new western and eastern borders that had been drawn to create a geographically truncated Pakistan, the terrible happenings there did not affect our city, and I had only vague inklings of the tension-filled atmosphere on the subcontinent.

On August 15, 1947, India, with new boundaries, became an independent nation. To commemorate the event, we had a special assembly at school the new national flag was raised and the singing of the national anthem was followed by distribution of sweets to all students. Soon after, I noticed train loads of displaced persons from West Pakistan, mostly from Sindh province, started pouring into Raipur for resettlement. At first, they were billeted in an abandoned army facility about 10 km outside the city. I visited the camp with a friend whose father was one of the volunteers looking after their basic needs. They all looked rather bewildered and shell shocked. However, it seems they were a very resilient and determined bunch, and soon the children of these displaced persons could be seen hawking cheap merchandize while jumping from carriage to carriage on moving trains, while many adults sold food and drinks from makeshift shacks on roadsides in and around the city.

One evening in January 1948, the world was shocked by the news that Mahatma Gandhi had been assassinated. I was at a friend's house attending his sister's wedding and the *Baraat* (groom's procession) was just arriving, led by a colourfully liveried musical band, when the news flash came on the radio. The music was immediately stopped and the wedding ritual was reduced to a bare minimum, in a very subdued atmosphere. The city became very tense with shops immediately closing their doors and the visible presence of law enforcement units. The tension did not ease until it was officially announced that the shooter was a Hindu fanatic and not a Muslim. The apostle of peace and non-violence was murdered because he refused to demonize a specific religious group for the communal upheaval following partition and insisted that the government of the newly independent India should transfer Pakistan's share of the treasury based on fairness and moral principles, rather than hold on to the funds for political and military expediency.

Nathuram Godsay, who shot Mahatma Gandhi, and his co-conspirators were found to have links with the RSS, and initially it was thought that the RSS organization may have had a hand in the assassination plot. The organization was banned and most of its high-level and many mid-level RSS members were put in jail, including some of the people I knew from my brief stint in the RSS. However, after a prolonged enquiry, an independent high-level commission, found that the conspirators, although affiliated with RSS, had acted independently and the RSS leadership had not played any direct role in the assassination plot. The ban on the RSS was ultimately lifted and over the years its influence has spread past its historic stronghold in Western India, especially to North and Central India where most of the displaced Hindus from West Pakistan had settled and continue to resent losing their ancestral homeland to Pakistan. Although the RSS claims to be a non-political organization, it has a strong influence on the Bharatiya Janata Party (BJP) which acts as the political arm of RSS and takes policy directions from it.

College years

In the spring of the year 1949, I took the final examinations for my high school certificate, which were conducted by the Provincial Board of Secondary Education, marking an important milestone in my early education. After spending a month with my cousins at my maternal uncle's house in the South, I returned to my ancestral home in Hatta where preparations were underway for the wedding of my eldest brother. As the wedding of the first male child in the family, the occasion had special significance, resulting in a larger than usual guest list and additional rituals, which extended the wedding celebrations from the usual three days to four days. In the middle of the wedding celebrations, I received a telegram from a friend in Raipur that the Provincial Board results had been published and that I had achieved the top position in the graduating class from our school, with especially high marks in science subjects. This news added another dimension to the joyful celebrations that were already underway.

Towards the end of the summer, we were again confronted with the decision about my future education. It was obvious that I should pursue a science program and based on economics and expediency, it was decided that I should enrol in the four-year Bachelor of Science course at the recently opened Government Science College at Raipur. So, at the beginning of the monsoon season, I was back in Raipur for another four years, living with my uncle who was now a family man with a wife and child. Our college was one of many post secondary institutions that sprung up after India's independence, as the country's new rulers placed increasing emphasis on education, in contrast to the British rulers who had little to gain from educating the Indian masses. Although I was enrolled in a curriculum with major emphasis on mathematics, physics, and chemistry, English and Hindi literature were still a compulsory part of the course work. The works I had to study included The Merchant of Venice, Pride and Prejudice and Matthew Arnold's long poem, Sohrab and Rustum – the story of conflict between a father and son from the Persian epic Shah Nama (Story of Kings) written by the tenth century poet Firdousi.

Until permanent buildings could be constructed, our classes were held in an abandoned army barrack with an asbestos roof. The science laboratories were housed in an old government office building that was assigned to the college. The facilities were very basic, with no space for a cafeteria or a common room where students could socialize. For out of town students, there were limited accommodations in makeshift residences consisting of a row of rental townhouses in the city. If I had been looking for the ambience of a well-established college or university campus, I would have been greatly disappointed. Sometimes it felt like I was in an unpaid 9-to-5 office job where I had to attend seminars all day. The college's limited facilities did not prevent me from making new friends and generally having a good time – although social interactions mostly took place outside the college campus, which was locked up after classes ended for the day.

Soon after I started college, the Army Medical Depot where my uncle worked finally shut its doors and he had to start looking for a new employer. Fortunately, it was not long before he was hired as a stenographer by the Income Tax Department, thus becoming a federal government employee.

This was a good move at least on two counts: first, it provided him with an opportunity for career advancement within the large bureaucracy, and second, as an Income Tax Department employee, he could expect occasional gifts from businessmen who were always looking for someone to help them navigate the labyrinthine bureaucracy of the Indian government, in general and the Income Tax Department, in particular. My uncle now had a wife and two children and I was happy that he not only had job security but also a reasonable chance for career advancement.

During the years that I lived with my uncle and aunt, we became very close; they always treated me and mine as part of their own family and have been very kind, generous and welcoming to us. My uncle inherited my ancestral home and he lived there for many years after he retired from the Income Tax Department. He passed away in 2007, and both Margaret and I regret profoundly that we were not able to visit him more often. As is customary in Indian families, my widowed aunt now lives with her elder son in another city, and our ancestral home in Hatta, where I spent my happy childhood, is empty, with no member of the Pandya family living in it any more.

Geo-politics of the time

After the turbulent times of the mid and late 1940s, the political and social atmosphere in India was stabilizing. India now had a new constitution which embodied the rights and freedoms of all citizens in a republic with a parliamentary system of democracy and universal adult franchise. The elected government of Prime Minister Jawaharlal Nehru was well established, with the first five-year plan for the development of agriculture, industry, and human resources underway. Most of the displaced persons from West Pakistan, a resilient and enterprising lot, had decided to move on with the business of building new lives for themselves. However, the picture was not so bright for the people displaced from East Bengal who were poorer to begin with and were ill-equipped to handle the struggles that faced them. When I landed in Calcutta in 1953, it was depressing to see many of these displaced families huddling around the railway stations and sidewalks of the city.

On the world stage, the Americans and their allies were nowhere close to wining the conflict in Korea against the communists and the Cold War was intensifying. India, as a newly independent and populous country, was being wooed by both sides. On one side, was the unrestricted capitalist approach, with everything open to the private sector and largely influenced by the Wall Street. On the other, was the highly restrictive communist approach, with everything, including people's day-to-day lives, controlled by the State? India finally opted for a mixed, socialist model with something from each one – a planned economy and state control of major industrial sectors, based on the Soviet model, and free speech, human rights, and open democracy from the American model, and declared itself as a member of a group of non-aligned nations. This model was successful in developing and sustaining a vibrant democracy, but was not so successful in promoting industrial growth, until the 1990s when the stifling bureaucratic controls were rapidly relaxed and the Indian entrepreneurial private sector was given a free hand.

From Raipur to Calcutta – journey continues

My time in Raipur came to an end in the spring of 1953 when I left for my hometown after writing the university examinations for the Bachelor of Science degree. At about the same time, my uncle and his family were getting ready to move to another city in the same region where he had been posted. I was not too unhappy to see the last of the city. Aesthetically, Raipur did not hold any attractions for me. It was like thousands of similar cities in India – featureless, functional at a basic level, and with little historical or cultural significance. On a personal level, my uncle's transfer to another place broke the only emotional ties I had with the city, and I had no personal connections except for a few college friends. I went home to spend the summer with my family and to see how my future was going to unfold. I had no definite plans and was hoping that as in the past, the stars would align in my favour and lead me to an interesting and rewarding career.

At the end of the summer, as the potential options were dwindling, I decided to join a graduate course in Chemical Engineering at a Technology Institute in the Provincial capital city of Nagpur and moved into the college residence there. Chemistry was not my strongest subject and I found the class and laboratory work hard. To my surprise, the stars decided to align in my favour after all, and within two weeks of starting the chemical engineering course, I received a telegram from my father informing me that I had been admitted to a three-year graduate course at the Institute of Radiophysics and Electronics at the

University of Calcutta and that I should proceed to Calcutta immediately. It was by sheer chance that I had come across the information about this Institute and put in an application, never imagining that it would bear fruit. It seems that the Institute was heavily funded by the federal government with the condition that at least six out of a class of twenty must be from provinces other than West Bengal. I was one of the six selected from rest of the country, against significant odds. During my three-year stay, there was only one other student from my province who came to the Institute in Calcutta. Strangely enough, he had also graduated from St. Paul's High School in Raipur, two years after me at the top of his class, and had attended the same college – he even ended up in Ontario, Canada teaching physics at McMaster University in Hamilton.

I quickly wound up my affairs in Nagpur, said goodbye to my roommate at the residence and boarded a train for the long journey to one of the largest (if not the largest) cities in the country. I knew only one person in Calcutta – a former classmate from high school with whom I had often played table tennis at the Railway Club and who was now enrolled in a college there to qualify as a homeopathic physician. I sent him a telegram informing him of my imminent arrival and had my fingers crossed with the fervent hope that he had received my telegram and would show up at the station to meet the train next morning and soften my landing in the unfamiliar mega city of Calcutta.

CHAPTER 5

A stranger in the mega city

As my train slowly pulled into Calcutta's enormous Howrah station in the morning, I was glued to the window, anxiously scanning the crowd of people on the platform, looking for my schoolmate, Giri. Finally, I spotted him and let out a sigh of relief that I would not have to tackle the strange city all on my own. After warm greetings, we started to make our way through the crowds towards the exit, following the red-shirted porter who was carrying my steel trunk and bedding. The scene outside was even more chaotic with a big jumble of taxis, cars, buses, trams and hand-pulled rickshaws and of course, masses of people going every which way. I could see the Howrah Bridge looming over the Hoogly River, a large estuary of the Ganges delta which empties into the Bay of Bengal. I could also see the sprawl of the mega city on the far bank of the Hoogly. Giri was kind enough to offer me temporary accommodation at his hostel until I could sort out the student residence options available from the University.

The first glimpse

Since I could not afford a taxi, we decided to take one of the privately-run buses, which, unlike the city-run buses in Calcutta, would accommodate my luggage. Eventually, the crowded bus made its way towards the entrance to the bridge and started rolling across the wide river towards the far bank. From my window, I could glimpse the Khidirpur docks on the Hoogly which is the main port in Calcutta for seagoing vessels – somewhat similar to the London docks on the Thames. These were perhaps the docks from which innumerable ships carrying indentured labourers sailed to distant lands and ships carrying bales of opium departed for China to supply the opium dens in that country. From the left window, I could see the building complex that houses the headquarters of the Ramkrishna Charitable Mission and Bellur temple built in memory of Swami

Ramkrishna Paramhans, who led the Hinduism's Reformation movement in the nineteenth century. His principal disciple, Swami Vivekanand, traveled to Chicago in 1893 and spoke at the World Parliament of Religions on the basic tenets of Hinduism and their roots in the ancient Vedantic texts. His subsequent travels, teachings, and writings on Vedantic view of life influenced many thinkers of the twentieth century, including Christopher Isherwood, Aldus Huxley and J. Krishnamurti.

The bus soon exited the Howrah Bridge and entered the city of Calcutta through a narrow street. This was a very congested area, full of shops and small businesses and mostly inhabited by Marwaris – a highly business-oriented community from the Rajasthan region who migrated in large numbers as traders during the British Raj. We got off the bus when it reached the end of this street, at the intersection with the Upper Circular Road, now known as State Highway 1 or simply SH1, across from the Sealdah Railway Station – the second largest railway station in Calcutta. Giri's hostel was close by, and we made our way there, carrying my belongings. The hostel was an old three-story building, with rooms built around an open courtyard with a veranda around it. Besides the entrance door, each room had a window opening onto the veranda and had no possibility of cross-ventilation. Given the normally humid weather in Calcutta and the absence of a ceiling fan in the rooms, I could hardly imagine the plight of the residents during the hot and humid nights. I was anxious to get to the University and register for the classes which were to start in a few days and to enquire about residence facilities. The Calcutta University College of Science and Technology was located further down from the hostel on the Upper Circular Road and, as it turned out, the Homeopathic College of Medicine and Hospital where Giri was enrolled was on the same road a few blocks further up from my destination. We had a quick bath, ate our morning meal of coarse rice and fish curry (the staple diet of Bengal) in the communal dining room, and took a bus to our respective destinations, arranging to meet at his college at the end of the day.

Settling in and exploring the mega-city

The campus of the University College of Science and Technology was dominated by the original building which accommodated some of the science departments. It was a large U-shaped, two-storey building, with a façade that reflected early twentieth century British Colonial architecture. The three technology departments and the Institute of Nuclear Physics were housed in separate buildings of a more recent vintage and were located at the back. In addition to a small cluster of administration buildings, there was a very small canteen for staff and students where one could buy tea and snacks, as well as simple meals. In keeping with Calcutta's high real estate prices and low availability, the campus was compact and physically walled in, with a single entrance gate. However, there was a distinct aura of academic activity on campus, with people working late into the evening in their offices and laboratories. The Department of Radiophysics and Electronics, where I was enrolled, was a modern two-storey building farthest from the campus entrance, and from the second floor of the building one could see the congested slum-like dwellings surrounding the campus walls at the back. When I enquired about possible accommodations in a university residence, I was happy to learn that a residence facility was available exclusively for the students of the technology departments who were admitted against seats reserved for students from outside West Bengal. I was given the address of the residence which was located on Ballygunge Circular Road, a fair distance from the college campus, and was advised to contact the residence supervisor.

After completing the registration formalities and spending some time with some of my other out-of-State prospective classmates, I made my way to the College of Homeopathic Medicine to meet my friend, Giri. That evening we met the resident supervisor and I was glad to learn that a place was available and I could move in the next evening. I was thankful for Giri's kind hospitality and assistance in guiding me around the city during those early days. We kept in touch regularly for the next two years while he completed his homeopathic medicine course and then returned home to join his father's homeopathic practice. I was glad to move into the residence because I was not looking forward to spending any more nights at the depressing hostel.

The Ballygunge neighbourhood was a rather upscale residential area. The residence was built on a piece of property owned by the University which housed its botany department and associated research plant nursery. Ballygunge Circular Road, on which the residence was located, was a wide tree-lined street with impressive homes on either side. These were occupied mainly by owners or high-level executives of large industrial or business enterprises. From our residence, we could see the large, gated villa belonging to Mr Thaper, an industrialist who owned a large number of jute mills. As we passed his estate on our way to catch public transport, we would see the Nepali *Durbaan* or gate keeper, sitting on a stool knitting sweaters or other woollen garments. This seemed to be a common practice for Nepali *Durbaans,* which kept them gainfully occupied between the sporadic interruptions necessary to attend to their duties.

The four-storey residence had been recently constructed. The first three floors were for student accommodations, while the dining hall and attached kitchen were located on the top floor. The rooms were bright and well ventilated with windows opening on two sides. I shared my third floor room with two other occupants. Each of us had a single platform bed, a desk with a built in bookshelf and a chair all made of sheet iron and painted a dirty green colour. In the absence of any closets or wardrobes, I had to keep my clothes, neatly folded in my steel trunk. The accommodations provided little privacy, not only from the people sharing the room, but also from other residents because the windows on one side opened onto the common passage which led to other rooms on the floor had no blinds or curtains. The residence fees included two meals a day in the dining room on the top floor. For an additional cost, one could also have morning and afternoon tea, with light snacks like toast (which always came with a sprinkling of sugar), boiled eggs, or omelettes, delivered to the room from the kitchen. The residence was primarily intended for students in the Technology Departments who had come from outside of West Bengal, so its population reflected the ethnic and linguistic diversity of India. In addition, it meant that English was most often the only common language amongst the residents. Although I was reasonably proficient in reading and writing English, I had had few occasions for engaging in extended conversations in the language, and welcomed this opportunity.

The prospect of living independently far away from home, without the protective presence of close family, marked my entry into early adulthood. Although I was excited at the prospect, I was also somewhat apprehensive about the unfamiliar environment and my ability to navigate successfully through the challenges it might present. However, the University term commenced in a few days and I started to develop friendships with some of the guys in my class as well as with other co-residents. Unlike me, a few of my out-of-province classmates had grown up and been educated in large cities such as Madras, Bombay and New Delhi and were not intimidated by the hustle and bustle of life in a mega city. Initially, I suffered from a bit of an inferiority complex when socializing with them because of my comparatively limited exposure to a cosmopolitan lifestyle. Mani, one of my classmates who became a good friend, had grown up in the

South Indian city of Madras and had graduated from a prestigious college there. His father was a high-level executive in the Indian Railways, posted to Calcutta and Mani lived with his family in a large apartment near Dhakuria Lake, within walking distance from our residence. Mani had a personality and a *joie de vivre* that I found fascinating, as well as he had interests that went beyond my own preferences for popular fiction, Bollywood movies and the latest Hindi songs. Mani was interested in the writings of modern philosophers, classical South Indian music and art. He introduced me to the writings of thinkers such as Nirad Chaudhari, Jean Paul Sartre, and Simone de Beauvoir. He also took me to the upstairs bar at the Lighthouse Theatre for my first alcoholic drink and told me to avoid certain areas of the Maidan, the large open grounds across the Grand Hotel in the heart of the city, after dark because it was frequented by gay men looking for partners. Diwan Mehta was another friend I made in Calcutta with whom I retained contact over many years. His family lived in Delhi after they had to flee their ancestral home on the eve of partition, and his account of their harrowing journey and some of the awful sights he had witnessed were highly disturbing.

Calcutta was originally a marshy village used as a trading post where the British East India Company built fortifications, mainly as a defence against the French who had a significant presence in India during the early days of the British East India Company. Calcutta became the capital of British India in 1772 after Robert Clive, a fortune hunter turned General, defeated Siraj-ud-daullah, the Nawab of Bengal, at the battle of Plassey. The first unplanned Indian attempt to revolt against the British rule, commonly referred to as the Indian Mutiny in the West, began in 1857 when the Indian soldiers in the British Indian army rebelled against the British rule. The revolt originated in Calcutta and quickly spread over most of North and Central India. After it was brutally put down by the British, the administration of India was transferred from the British East India Company to the British Crown. The British had a great deal of influence on the development and planning of the city, on the architectural style of its major landmarks, and on the education and cultural lives of its indigenous population. The capital of British India was eventually moved to Delhi in 1911, where the British architect Luytens designed the part of the city now called New Delhi to accommodate the bureaucracy of the British Raj. Delhi is a very old city and was the seat of so many ruling dynasties that it is sometimes referred to as the 'graveyard of empires'. True to its reputation, in less than four decades the British

Ensign was permanently lowered from Delhi's Red Fort on August 15, 1947 and the British Empire joined many of its predecessors in the graveyard.

When I arrived in Calcutta in 1953, it was the largest city in India and eighth largest in the world. It had only been six years since the British had left, and the city had not yet shed the British influence to any noticeable extent. Calcutta was still Calcutta and not Kolkata, Howrah Bridge was still Howrah Bridge and not Rabindra Setu, Dalhousie Square had not yet been renamed B.B.D. Park and there was no Mahatma Gandhi Road or Jawahar Lal Nehru Road. The British era Grand Hotel and the Great Eastern Hotel were still the only two Western style hotels in town. There were no skyscrapers and the City Metro had not been imagined. I loved taking the streetcar to the city centre, which was called simply Chauranghee and Esplanade, to watch an English movie at the popular Lighthouse Theatre or grab a snack and tea at the Annapoorna, a large cafeteria run by an organization of widows. Most of the major landmarks were built around the Maidan, a vast open space spreading from the Victoria Memorial at one end to the Ochterloney Monument at the other, with sports clubs, playing fields and picnic areas in the middle. In addition to the Victoria Memorial and the Ochterlony Monument, other architectural landmarks from the British era close to the Maidan included: Eden Gardens, one of the largest Cricket stadiums in the world; the High Court; the Governor General's residence, the Writers building, where scores of Bengali Babus or clerks toiled for the British Raj.

The New Market, which housed a vast collection of shops selling a wide range of goods, frequented by rich Indian and Western shoppers, was also located nearby. A number of English theatres and the United States Information Service (USIS) library and reading room were also located in this area. The USIS library, with its floor-to-ceiling plate glass windows, was always an attractive target for stone throwing left-wing demonstrators. However, the air conditioned USIS reading room was also a convenient place to drop in for a brief respite from the heat and humidity while waiting to meet a friend or for appointments in the area. When it came to borrowing books or spending an evening listening to invited speakers, I preferred the British Council Library which was located in a small villa-like building surrounded by nice gardens on Shakespeare Street branching off Park Street. Park Street was a beautiful tree-lined street with Edwardian buildings, similar to an elegant residential area of London. At one end of Park Street, there is the old English cemetery, with graves dating back to the early eighteenth century, which was a popular destination for genealogists looking for ancestors who had passed away in Calcutta in the service of the British Raj and were interned in this old cemetery.

For a young man away from home, life in Calcutta was interesting and exciting. Living in an upscale residential part of the city, populated by mostly upper-middle class Bengali *Bhadra Lok* (gentle folk), was a new experience. In the evening, my friends and I would often walk down to Rashbihari Avenue, the main thoroughfare in Ballygunge, to watch the well-dressed Bengali girls out shopping or strolling. We would make comments on the girls' physical attributes to one another – a common pastime for young men in India in those days. I also enjoyed browsing for used books in the second-hand book stalls lining College Street near the Presidency College, established in 1817, and the University of Calcutta, established in 1857. At the time, my recreational reading ran to the adventures of Bertie Wooster and Jeeves, the escapades of Simon Templar, a.k.a. the Saint, and the courtroom antics of Perry Mason.

In terms of my day-to-day routine, life at the residence was generally pleasant except for the unfamiliar local cuisine and questionable quality of the food. I tried the local diet of fish curry and rice but was frustrated by the unusually large number of fish scales in the popular Hilsa fish which was served with most meals. Fortunately, within a year, a Sikh entrepreneur opened a restaurant at a nearby intersection, where we caught the bus or streetcar, which served North Indian food. Some of us who were unhappy with the residence food were able to negotiate a deal with the manager to have morning and evening meals at the restaurant for a reasonable monthly charge. The restaurant had a number of booths, more like cabins, each with a colourful curtain. These attracted many young lovers who would often bribe the waiter to give them some private time behind the curtain. There was also a *Dhaba* (shack) nearby which we frequented for tea and snacks in the afternoon when taking a break from the long hours of studying for our University examinations.

Impressions of Bengali culture

I soon learned that the Bengalis were very proud and protective of their language, literature, and culture. Unlike Western and Northern India, Bengal was generally well-shielded from frequent invasions which mostly came from the north-west, as well as from prolonged, recurring local conflicts. The Bengalis benefited from these long periods of peace and stability and developed a highly cohesive and cultured society. The introduction of Western secular ideas and education, starting in the early nineteenth century, gave rise to social and religious reformation movements, such as the Brahmo Samaj and Vedantic path – the former spearheaded by Raja Ram Mohan Roy and the latter by Swami Vivekanand, both from Calcutta. As well, the influence of the revered Nobel Laureate Rabindra Nath Tagore on Bengali literature, music, and art is pervasive throughout West Bengal and Bangladesh, which was part of Bengal before partition. Tagore has the unique distinction of being the author of the national anthems of not one, but two independent countries – India and Bangladesh. Bengal's two major festivals *Durga Pooja* and *Saraswati Pooja* always include the recitation of Tagore's poetry sung in the musical style he developed, called Rabindra Sangeet.

Although *Durga Pooja* is also celebrated in other parts of India under various names, such as *Durgaashtmi Navaratri, Dussehra,* for Bengalis, wherever they may be, *Durga Pooja* represents the most important festival of the year. This is the time when individuals, families and communities honour *Durga,* the Hindu goddess which represents the divine female energy. The communal celebrations extend over seven to eight days and each local community usually erects a large marquee which serves as a temporary temple where a clay image of goddess *Durga* is prominently displayed. It becomes the focus of religious rituals, as well as cultural events that are part of the celebrations by the community at large. In the evening, families and groups of people walk from one display to another, marvelling at the workmanship of the various clay sculptures of the goddess and sampling the cultural programs at each location. Nirad C. Chaudhari, in his book Autobiography of an Unknown Indian, provides a very detailed and vivid description of the *Durga Pooja* celebrations in rural Bengal, including sacrifices of goats as part of the religious rituals. For many of us, to observe and participate in the *Durga Pooja* celebrations in Calcutta, especially in South Calcutta where our residence was located, was a grand religious and cultural experience.

Saraswati Pooja, which honours *Saraswati,* the Hindu goddess of learning and arts, is a uniquely Bengali tradition, and is generally organized and enthusiastically celebrated by the Bengali student communities in and outside of Bengal. This festival has a special significance for the students and staff of educational and cultural institutions, and all reasonably sized institutions in the city organized their own celebrations to honour the goddess of learning and arts. At our residence, each of us contributed towards the purchase of a clay idol of

Saraswati, who is always depicted sitting on a lotus flower playing a *Veena,* a sitar-like stringed instrument, and we erected a temporary marquee in the forecourt of the residence for the duration of the celebrations, which continued late into the night for several days. At the end of the *Durga Pooja* and the *Saraswati Pooja* celebrations, the clay idols from all over the city were placed on decorated floats and paraded through the streets with a lot of fanfare, and finally immersed in the Hoogly River.

Sad good bye to an exciting phase

On the academic front, I was very happy and felt privileged to be studying topics that were at the forefront of technology at the time, such as wired and wireless communications, electronics, and the principles of digital computing. By today's standards, the devices, systems and applications were primitive, to say the least, but the underlying science is still the same and it was exciting at the time. Except for the telegraph and telephone systems that used electro-mechanical relays and the radio and TV sets that used vacuum tubes, there were few obvious civilian applications for the rapidly emerging advances in electronics, communications and computer technologies. World War II had led to a quantum advance in these technologies, mainly to develop military applications for communication, command and control of force deployments over land, air and water for offence and defence purposes. A significant part of the research was carried out at the Radiation Laboratories at MIT in the United States, and after the war, had been declassified and published in more than twenty volumes as the Radiation Laboratory Series (RLS). There were only a handful of text books on the subjects we were studying and the ones that were available were not very satisfactory. One exception was a book on Radio Engineering by Professor F.E. Terman of Stanford University, many of whose students, including Hewlett and Packard, became pioneers in electronics, communications and computers. The Radiation Laboratory volumes became our main source of information and reference for our courses. We have come a long way from those early days, and the related technologies have advanced to unimaginable levels. Their emerging applications have become so embedded in our daily lives that we can hardly imagine living in today's society without easy access to them.

The first two years of the three-year course were the toughest because we covered a lot of ground on the underlying mathematics and physics of the technologies, as well as their contemporary applications. In our third year, we were allowed to choose from a number of specialized areas and did not have to cover too wide a spectrum. The University still operated on the outdated notion of written examinations once every year or once every two years which meant that we had a gruelling examination at the end of our first two years of study, and another one at the end of our third year. Since the course material that was covered in the first two years was very extensive, preparing for the examination was physically and mentally very demanding. Fortunately, the examinations were scheduled after the summer vacation, which meant that we had two months to spend preparing for the upcoming test of our physical endurance and capacity to retain a massive amount of information. It also meant that we had to spend our vacation at the residence, glued to our books instead of going home to enjoy the break. During the examinations, it was not uncommon for a student to get discouraged and drop out if he did poorly on one or two tests and was afraid of getting a low overall grade. The hope was that he would do better next year, and the loss of one year was worth the chance of getting a better grade upon graduation from the University. This happened to one of my friends and roommates at the residence. He came back after a discouraging performance in the day's test and was seriously considering dropping out and wasting a year. We spent the better part of the evening trying to talk him out of taking such a drastic step. Fortunately, he decided to continue taking the rest of the tests. He finally graduated with good grades, and eventually earned a doctorate from Berkley, becoming a distinguished professor at the University of California and the recipient of many prestigious national and international academic awards and honours.

In July of 1956, I wrote the final examinations for my post-graduate degree and said goodbye to Calcutta, hoping to return some day, but unfortunately, that was not to be. To finish my degree, I had to complete a period of on-the-job training in a relevant organization. The University was responsible for arranging the placement of its graduating students as interns once it was determined that he or she had successfully passed the written examinations. This process could take anywhere from two to three months, so I had no option but to return to my ancestral home and wait for the placement letter to arrive from the university. The three years that I had spent in Calcutta provided me with the opportunity not only to earn a post-graduate degree in a rapidly evolving discipline, but also to mature as an independent adult. The exposure to Calcutta's urban cosmopolitan environment helped to round off some of the rough edges of my small-town background. I enjoyed my stay in Calcutta and made a number of good friends from various parts of India. My one regret was that I failed to take advantage of the opportunity to become fluent in the rich Bengali language and missed the pleasure of reading outstanding Bengali authors like Rabindra Nath Tagore and Bankim Chandra Chatterjee in their original language, and enjoying movies by Satyajit Ray without English subtitles.

CHAPTER 6

A year under the shadow of the Taj Mahal

I arrived home with little idea about when or where I would travel next. Over the past three years I had only been home for short periods during some of the university holidays and had lost contact with most of my boyhood friends who had either moved away for university education or taken up jobs in larger towns and cities. Although people in town who had known me from my childhood were very friendly, there was little common ground for any sustained social interaction and intellectual dialogue beyond exchanging pleasantries. I had travelled too far physically, as well as academically, and had outgrown the environment that had nurtured me as a young boy. My parents and family members were glad that I was able to spend a long period of time at home. Typically, in an extended Indian family, close family members come and go at their own convenience as a matter of right, so my presence was neither an occasion for celebration nor an unwelcome intrusion. I slipped into the role of the youngest son of the family with little fanfare, and enjoyed the simple home-cooked meals served with love and affection by my grandmother, my mother and my sisters.

It was the middle of the monsoon season and the landscape was full of vegetation, the river and ponds were full of water, and the streets were full of mud. At night one could hear the mating symphony of the frogs that made their home in the ponds near our house. I spent most of the time going for long walks in the morning and evening, revisiting my boyhood haunts in areas surrounding the town, or reading any Hindi or English books that I could lay my hands on. I was fortunate that a neighbour who had just completed an M.A. in English literature was in town waiting to find a job. He generously loaned me books from his collection, which included novels by Oscar Wilde, Charles Dickens, A.J. Cronin, and John Steinbeck. I also came across the highly readable books of Alexander Dumas (and his ghost writers) and devoured his famous adventure tales, including The Three Musketeers, The Man in the Iron Mask, The Black Tulip, and The Count of Monte Cristo.

In the middle of September, I finally received a letter from the University advising me that an intern's position has been secured for me at the Army Electrical and Mechanical Engineering (EME) Workshop, located in the city of Agra. The one-year position included a modest monthly stipend for living expenses and I was to report for work before the end of the month. Agra, known worldwide as the location of the famous Taj Mahal, is a historic city where a number of *Mugal* Emperors, made their residence. In addition to the Taj Mahal, the city is full of historic sights from the *Mugal* period. I was very excited at the prospect of spending a year in Agra and visiting the historic sights in and around the city. I was also looking forward to applying the scientific and technical knowledge that I had acquired over the years to real-world applications.

On a morning in late September, I arrived at the Agra train station. I was a complete stranger to the city, with no local friends or acquaintances who could introduce me to the city. After depositing my bedding roll and the steel trunk at the left-luggage office at the train station, I hired a bicycle rickshaw to take me to the EME Workshop which was about five kilometres from the station, in the southern outskirts of the city. As I reached the entrance to my destination, the first thing I saw was a large shed, chock full of bicycles which I assumed were the main transport used by the Workshop employees. At the security gate, I showed the appointment letter from the University and, after signing my name and time of arrival, I was escorted to the administrative offices – a single storey barrack with well-tended flower beds around it. There, an Army Captain briefed me about the structure and general mandate of this particular EME Workshop, which was one of a number of similar establishments scattered through the country, and my role and responsibilities as an intern. The Workshop was staffed mainly by civilians, with only a few dozen uniformed commissioned and non-commissioned officers in supervisory positions. I was then escorted to another building which housed the maintenance activities for the electrical and electronics equipment used by the Indian Army. I was handed over to a Non Commissioned Officer (NCO) who was to be my supervisor for the first of a series of rotations through different departments at the Workshop. The NCO walked me through the facilities and showed me some of the equipment that this department was responsible for maintaining. The equipment ranged from simple walkie-talkies used by the soldiers in the field to World War II vintage anti-aircraft radar units.

My immediate priority was to find suitable and affordable accommodation in the vicinity of the Workshop. To this end, I sought advice from my supervisor. He told me that there were a few other graduates from a local engineering college who were also employed as interns at the Workshop who might be able to help me. Fortunately, one of them, a young Punjabi mechanical engineering graduate, was renting a room in the cantonment area of the city and agreed to share accommodations with me. I was able to move in with him that same evening. The room was one of a dozen rooms for rent on the second floor of a small shopping plaza on the main north-south inter-city highway. The establishments on the ground floor included a doctor's office, a bicycle rental shop, a *Hallwai* and a general store. The building itself was in the middle of a typical Indian Bazaar, with stalls selling all manner of goods and services. The rental rooms were arranged like the second floor of a cheap motel, with each room opening to a narrow common walkway which led to a large terrace where we slept during the hot summer nights. The rooms were bare, with no running water and a single naked electric bulb as the only source of light at night. There was a communal water tap downstairs that we used for bathing and for drinking water. However, the location was very convenient. Besides being close to a movie house, the India Coffee House and the somewhat upscale shops on the main cantonment road, it was also within a couple of miles of the Taj Mahal and the Red Fort.

With my roommate's help, I rented a bicycle from the bicycle shop downstairs and arranged for lunch and dinner at a nearby vegetarian restaurant. My roommate originally came from the western part of Punjab and his family had to move from Pakistan during the partition. He had graduated from the local engineering college and was well acquainted with Agra and its surroundings. He was also an avid reader of English fiction, with special fondness for the stories of the American Wild West and the exploits of famous cowboys described by Zane Gray and other writers of that genre. Fortunately, the neighbourhood movie house often featured Western movies on Sunday mornings. A group of us became regular patrons at these Sunday morning screenings, and greatly enjoyed such Western classics as High Noon, Billy the Kid and Gunfight at the O.K. Corral.

Our weekday routine was simple. In the morning, a young boy brought us tea and toast from a nearby tea shop. Next, we bicycled the three kilometres to the Army Workshop. We were allowed short morning and afternoon tea breaks, plus an hour-long break at midday, during which we bicycled back to the restaurant near our residence for lunch. After work, a few of us generally wandered down to the India Coffee House for coffee and conversation. Talk centred on politics, movies, books, and our actual or imagined romantic encounters with the opposite sex, past and present and ribald jokes and stories. The India Coffee Houses were probably the first chain restaurants to spring up like mushrooms in major towns and cities in India, in the early 1950s. They were established by an association of coffee growers and workers in Southern India, mostly from Kerala Province, to popularize coffee in Northern India, where tea was the drink of choice. They served excellent coffee, as well as South Indian snacks like *dosa, idli, wada,* and *sambar* and soon became a popular place for young people to hang out and indulge in informal discussions and gossip.

The Anglo-Indian community

One of the neighbours in our rooming complex became a regular member of our Coffee House group. He was a little older than us, and was a civilian employee at a local military establishments. He had become close friends with an Anglo-Indian family in town and was romantically involved with their youngest daughter. The romance had to be conducted in a clandestine fashion because there were no open venues where young people could mix freely and pursue their romantic liaisons so that these romantic encounters mostly consisted of stolen kisses, groping in dark corners and writing secret love letters. Besides relishing the torrid details of the romance which the friend described, most likely with some embellishments, I was also interested in gaining a better understanding of the Anglo-Indian community in India. The largest Anglo-Indian community lived in Calcutta and during my three-year stay there I frequently saw Anglo-Indians in the Chaurrangi and Park Street areas. However, I had never had any social interaction with members of this community and knew little about their lifestyle and culture. My curiosity was further fuelled by John Masters' novel Bhowani Junction and its movie version which captured the plight of the community at the departure of British Raj. The story details the dilemma of a young Anglo-Indian woman, played by Ava Gardner in the film, who is trying to find her place in a country and society on the cusp of major changes. Through our neighbour, I became acquainted with his girlfriend's family and was able to get a better understanding of the trials and tribulations faced by the Anglo-Indian community and the family's struggles to find a place where they would not face constant discrimination and isolation.

The relatively small, mixed-race community of Anglo-Indians in India was the product of sexual encounters between British men and mostly lower class Indian women during the British presence in India over two centuries. Unfortunately, the community had a very difficult time finding its place within the social structures of India during and immediately after the British Raj. On the one hand, the British in India and in Britain considered Anglo-Indians to be socially inferior and declined to socialize with them or take any practical steps towards looking after their welfare, except for giving them some preference in low and mid level jobs in the Indian Railways, and a few other Security related services. The practice was abolished when India gained independence. Most of the Anglo-Indians generally identified themselves as more British than Indian and did not feel comfortable assimilating with the so called 'Natives'. They further alienated themselves from the majority population by siding with the British during the Indian independence movement.

The Anglo-Indian community existed on the periphery, having very little social interaction with the larger Indian society or the members of the British ruling class in India. They continued to consider England as their 'home' country – although few Anglo-Indians had ever set foot in England – and considered English their mother tongue. They also tried to imitate the British in terms of food, dress, and other social customs, including a less restrictive attitude towards intermingling of the sexes, mostly within their own community. Sadly, in the absence of any tangible ties with British history or culture, the imitation degenerated into a somewhat pathetic parody. Fortunately, when countries like Britain, Canada and Australia relaxed their immigration requirements, Anglo-Indian families took advantage and immigrated to these countries in large numbers so that currently there are more Anglo-Indians living abroad than in India itself. It seems they have finally found societies that are more inclusive, less judgemental and generally more welcoming of diverse cultures and ethnicities.

The Radha Swami sect

My roommate would often invite me to accompany him on the weekend to his *alma mater* located in a suburb called Dayaal Baag, to visit with his college friends who were still living at the campus. We would bicycle down there to spend the day visiting friends and wandering around the community and participating in their sports and cultural activities. Dayaal Baag is a self-contained community and satellite town located about 10 kilometres north of the Agra city centre. It was established in 1915 by one of the spiritual leaders of the *Radha Swami* sect of Hindus, whose members are commonly referred as *Satsangis*. The *Radha Swami* faith presents itself as a natural, contemporary and scientific religion, devoid of rites, rituals, ceremonies and dogmas. It is based on self experience and self alleviation for self realization or salvation, under the guidance of a living Spiritual Master. The guiding ideals are *Bhakti* (devotion), faith, dedication, discipline, humility, modesty/simplicity, austerity and a firm belief in the supremacy of God and brotherhood of human beings. *Satsangis* are strictly vegetarian, reflecting a philosophy of respect for all living things, and they abstain from alcohol and highly spiced food that may interfere with their daily meditation and spiritual life. Many of its teachings are similar to those of other proponents of the *Bhakti* as path to salvation, such as Mira Bai, Kabir, Guru Nanak and Rumi, the Persian poet.

The charitable trust associated with the sect has established educational institutions around India for the education of boys and girls. My own interest and curiosity about the *Radha Swami* sect was based on the fact that my father's last teaching job, before he returned permanently to his ancestral home, was at a middle school operated by the *Radha Swami* sect in Timarni, a small town in Central India. Undoubtedly, I must have overheard discussions among family and friends about the *Radha Swami* sect and developed some curiosity about their world view. I was therefore glad that I could spend some time at their major spiritual centre and appreciate the cultural richness of this model colony, which showcased their devotion to their principles and approach to life, and to living in harmony with nature. Dayaal Bag's close proximity to the city of Agra means that Agra not only attracts visitors to see the Taj Mahal and various other historic *Mugal* era monuments, but also attracts people from all over the country and abroad who visit Dayaal Baag as a spiritual pilgrimage.

Search for suitable employment

During my year in Agra, I spent many afternoons at the Taj Mahal, not as a tourist, but as a resident taking advantage of a local venue for a pleasant afternoon. After lunch on Sundays, if the weather was nice, I would frequently bicycle down to the Taj Mahal, taking along a book. I would find a quiet spot on a covered terrace on one of the outbuildings and spend a few hours reading and admiring the beauty of the Taj, whose marble façade would be shimmering in the sun, and enjoying the peace and serenity of the formal gardens that face the monument. From my perch on one of the open lookout windows surrounding the second-floor terrace, I could observe the tourists and visitors wandering through the Taj Mahal and its gardens, as well as the surrounding countryside and the massive Red Fort along the bend on the Yamuna River. The builder of the Taj Mahal, Emperor Shahjahan, was imprisoned by his son and successor, Aurangzeb, in the Red Fort, where he spent his last days as a broken old man. Legend has it that he spent many hours sitting on his little balcony, longing for his beloved wife, Mumtaj Mahal, while gazing at the Taj Mahal, the monument he built as a token of his love for her – a monument which is not only an architectural marvel but also a universal symbol of eternal love and loyalty. At the time, little did I imagine that within half a dozen years, I would return to the Taj Mahal on my own honeymoon with my Canadian bride, who would be amazed at the sheer beauty of this monument immortalizing an emperor's love for his wife

By early spring one of my pressing concerns was to secure a more permanent position in line with my educational qualifications. In those days the prevailing wisdom was to strive for a suitable Central or Provincial government job. These were considered to provide stable, lifelong employment, with a reasonable salary and retirement benefits. The flipside was the stagnation and boredom that result from a bureaucratic environment where advancement is tied to the number of years an individual has spent in the job and his/her connections within the higher echelons of bureaucracy or political elite, rather than the individual's ability, drive and job performance. Under Prime Minister Nehru's socialistic approach to economic development, governments had a controlling hand in most of my areas of interest, and jobs in my field in the private sector were few and far between. This meant I had little choice but to keep an eye out for suitable entry-level jobs in government departments, such as Radio Broadcasting, Civil Aviation, government-funded research labs and Engineering Education. The selection process for these jobs was highly centralized and top-heavy in its approach, with the line managers or supervisors having no say in the selection of candidates. The interview board generally consisted of a bunch of bureaucrats on the permanent selection board for all government positions with one or two technical experts, with no voting powers, invited to sit in.

I kept applying for jobs as I saw them advertised in the daily newspapers, and soon began to receive invitations for job interviews. The places I travelled to for job interviews included Bombay, Delhi, and Simla, the last being a hill station in the foot hills of the Himalayas that had been the summer capital of the British administration in India. To attend these interviews, I was generally entitled to an economy class return train fare and a small daily allowance which barely covered the cost of meals. Prospective interviewees were left to their own devices to find accommodation for the overnight stays – which we managed mostly by imposing on our friends or acquaintances at the destination. My first interview was for a job at a Research Lab in Bombay. I had never been to Bombay before and I had no friends or acquaintances there that could provide me with overnight shelter. I was hoping to find accommodation in a *Dharamsala*, and in the worst case, I knew I could spend the night at the railway station, like thousands of others, and check my belongings at the 'left luggage' office before finding my way to the interview location, at the Bombay Yacht Club right next to the famous Gateway of India and the Taj Hotel.

Fortunately, on the train to Bombay I ran into an acquaintance from my hometown who was also travelling to Bombay for a job interview (for a different job), and he invited me to stay with him in his cousin's vacant apartment. This not only solved my pressing accommodation problem, but also enabled me to stay in Bombay for a couple of extra days of sightseeing. The second floor apartment was located above an Irani restaurant. These Irani restaurants were a very common sight on busy intersections in Bombay. Unfortunately, I do not think I made a very good impression at this first job interview. I was nervous and somewhat self-conscious about my lack of appropriate interview attire – I did not own a jacket or a tie and was dressed in rather informal clothes. After the job interview, I spent a few pleasant days exploring the city with my host. I was impressed by the highly cosmopolitan mix of the population and the energy and drive of the city's residents. Although I did not get the job, the trip to Bombay did have an indirect influence on my life. It was on my return trip from Bombay that I met and befriended a young man from Toronto, Canada on his travels around the world. He was on his way to Agra to see the Taj Mahal and I invited him to stay with me and we spent the next few days together. This brief contact brought Canada into my consciousness and later influenced my decision to choose Canada and Toronto as my preference for graduate studies – and, the rest, as they say, is history.

The next two interviews took place in the summer. The first was in Delhi for the position of a maintenance engineer for electronic equipment used by the Civil Aviation Authority. By now, I was a bit better prepared for the interviews – I had even borrowed a tie from a neighbor and learned to tie it – and I was satisfied with my performance. I arrived in Delhi on a hot summer evening and in the absence of pre-arranged lodging decided to spend the night at a *Dharamsala* near the New Delhi Railway station. The *Dharamsala* was a single-storey building consisting of several small rooms arranged around a large open courtyard with a few trees. The only furniture in the room was a *Charpoy* string bed. As is common in the summer months in Northern India, most residents moved their beds into the open courtyard for the night because the heat inside the rooms would have been unbearable. In the middle of the night, I got extremely thirsty and, in desperation, I looked around and noticed that the person sleeping on the next bed had a *Surahi*, an earthen water container that travelers carry in summer, next to his bed. Rather than waking him in the middle of the night, I stealthily helped myself to a glass of water from his water container. The next morning when I woke up I noticed that the neighbor whose water I had shared looked rather under the weather. I did not pay much attention to this until I was back in Agra the next day and started to experience serious symptoms of the Hong Kong flu that was spreading fast everywhere

After having breakfast at a food stall near the railway station, I proceeded to find my way to the interview site in New Delhi – the part of Delhi planned and designed by Luytens more than fifty years ago to accommodate the British Raj and all its administrative trappings. It had been only ten years since the British had left India and New Delhi and its business centre, the Connaught Circus, still had a very Western look and feel. This has gradually disappeared with the unimaginative planning and construction of post-independence high rise structures, as well as the unprecedented growth in population, which began with the massive influx of displaced persons into Delhi as a result of the partition of the country. When I reached the venue for the interview, I was happy to see the familiar faces of a few classmates and friends from Calcutta among the prospective candidates waiting to be interviewed. My good friends Mani and Mehta were among them and we made plans to spend the afternoon and evening together, exploring the sights and sounds of Delhi. The interview itself lasted for no more than fifteen minutes and I was generally satisfied with my performance and hoped to be included in the list of successful candidates for one of the available positions. However, I knew that I might have to wait for a long time before I would hear the final result because the Government bureaucracy moved at a snail's pace, if at all.

As a first time visitor to Delhi, I was impressed by the colonial era buildings and the beautifully planned and well maintained residential areas of New Delhi with their wide tree-lined avenues. Having been the capital of many ruling dynasties, the greater Delhi area is a fascinating amalgam of modernity and antiquity. There are two principal components in this mixture. One is the mark of the British, seen in such twentieth century structures as the President's residence, the former residence of the British Viceroy, and the Parliament House. These buildings face each other across a wide avenue with huge lawns on either side, with the India Gate sitting in the middle, rather like the National Mall in Washington DC. Connaught Place, the main shopping and business centre, is another concrete reminder of the British colonial era. It consists of buildings with wide arched arcades arranged around a large circular space with wide radial avenues branching off in various directions. The second prominent component reflects the Islamic dynasties that preceded the British and ruled from Delhi for many centuries. While travelling along a wide modern avenue it is not uncommon to suddenly come across such Islamic contributions as Emperor Humayun's tomb, the Lodi Gardens, Hauz Khas and Jantar Mantar, a seventeenth century astronomic observatory located within a stone's throw from Connaught Place.

Within a few weeks of my return from Delhi, I was invited to an interview for a position with All India Radio, the sole radio broadcasting network in India operated by the Ministry of Information – there were no private radio stations and no television broadcasting in the country at the time. The interview was to be held at Simla, a hill station in the foothills of the Himalayas that had been used as the summer headquarters of the civil and military administration of the British Raj during the hottest months of the year. For almost a century, Simla had been the most sought after summer resort for the higher echelons of the British society in India – a place where they could relax the traditional stiff upper lip a little and let down their hair. In its hay day, Simla acquired a reputation as a hotbed of adultery, or at least gossip about adultery. Rudyard Kipling, who spent some time there around 1907, is quoted as saying that Simla had a reputation for "frivolity, gossip and intrigue". No wonder one of the most popular tourist spots in Simla is called 'Scandal Point.' After the British left and air conditioners became more readily available, the practice of moving the capital to Simla during the summer was abandoned.

I had never been to a hill station and Simla had the reputation of being one of the best planned hill stations in India, so I was keenly looking forward to my short visit there at the Government's expense. I took a night train to a place called Kalka, northwest of Delhi, and boarded the narrow gauge toy train to Simla the next morning. The 100 km journey from Kalka to Simla was a once in a lifetime experience and is perhaps my most memorable train journey. While the train journey through the Canadian Rockies is very scenic and enjoyable, this little toy train's struggle to climb from the Indo-Gangetic plains to a height of almost 8,000 feet in the Himalayas with a track length of less than 100 km is unforgettable. Later, when I had an opportunity to read the children's classic 'The Little Engine that Could,' it reminded me of the little steam engine on our train to Simla valiantly making its way up the steeply climbing route through the Himalayan mountains. The train route was completed in 1906, and consists of over 100 tunnels, 800 bridges, and 900 switchbacks. This narrow gauge train route has now been declared a UNESCO World Heritage Structure as an example of a great engineering accomplishment.

As the train climbed slowly through frequent twists and turns into the higher altitudes, I observed the changes unfolding in the terrain and the scenery, as well as in the foliage and trees that formed the dense woods and forests on the hills. For the first time in my life, I saw coniferous trees with their sculpted shapes, unfamiliar foliage, and smelt the distinctive fragrance of pine needles. It took the toy train almost six hours to complete the 100 km journey and it arrived at the small, quaint railway station in Simla in the mid-afternoon. I was glad that my friends, Mani and Mehta, who had been invited to the same job interview, were there to meet me. They were staying in a cheap guesthouse in the lower bazaar which had been mostly inhabited by the 'natives' during the British Raj and consisted of narrow alleys crowded with small shops, food stalls, and strange dwellings. The guesthouse, a simple structure completely made of wood, hugged the side of a hill on a steeply climbing narrow lane.

The first thing I noticed on my arrival in Simla was the quality of the air. It was cool, crisp, and clean compared to the usual summer temperatures of over 45C that I had left behind in Agra, where blowing dust constantly attacked your exposed skin. On experiencing this soothing and serene atmosphere for the first time, I could not fault the British men and their mem sahibs in India for retreating to hill stations like Simla during the summer months rather than suffer the unpleasant heat and dust on the plains. Simla, as I found out in the next couple of days, was well planned and well laid out as an exclusive place for the British gentry to escape and indulge in their nostalgia for 'home' and try to replicate the fun and romance that they missed. They made sure that all of the major public and administrative buildings had a distinct British look and the residential bungalows were well spaced around the upper ridges, away from the local population. Most of the public buildings were scattered along the pedestrian mall which was almost 6 km long and formed the focus of most socio-economic activities, with shops, restaurants, coffee and tea houses, hotels, and theaters along both sides. Strolling along the mall in the evening is part of the daily ritual for residents and visitors alike. The most prominent building in Simla is the residential mansion for the Viceroy – a five-storey structure in neo-gothic style surrounded by extensive grounds and gardens. It is one of the very few stone structures built by the British in Simla and is now used to house the Indian Institute of Advanced Studies. Canadian author M.G. Vassanji, who spent some time as a guest scholar at the Institute of Advanced Studies in Simla, provides an interesting description of contemporary Simla and its environs in his travelogue The Place Within.

When I returned from my brief sojourn in cool, beautiful Simla to the heat and dust of Agra, I learned that my roommate had been offered an entry-level position at one of the largest hydro-electric projects in India, located in his home province of Punjab. He left for his new job just before the monsoons broke in North India in their full glory, bringing long awaited relief from the heat and turning the landscape overnight from the drab and dirty brown shades of the summer to a lush green. By this time, my original circle of friends had depleted as many of them found new jobs and moved away. I was starting to feel restless and was looking forward to securing a permanent position which would offer some stability and a career path that I could pursue. The end of my one-year term as an intern was fast approaching, and I still had no definite job offer, although I had a few irons in the fire and was awaiting responses from my interviews.

At the end of September 1957, a few weeks before I was due to leave Agra, I learned that a teaching position was open in the Electronics and Telecommunications Department at the Engineering College located in Jabalpur, the city of my birth. The college had been established in 1948 by the Provincial Government soon after India gained independence and was the only engineering college in our province. It was also one of the very few institutions in India at the time which offered undergraduate and graduate courses in electronics and telecommunications. The successful candidate was to be selected on an *ad hoc* basis, without a formal open competition, by the provincial education ministry which funded and oversaw the operation of the engineering college. I sent in my application, confident that I was more than qualified for the position. However, knowing the ways of the entrenched government bureaucracy, I knew that a successful outcome within a reasonable time could only be achieved by one or more personal visits to the powers-that-be at Bhopal, the provincial capital, as well as by mobilizing any personal contacts that could help in securing a favorable and expeditious decision.

I wound up my affairs in Agra and took the night train to Bhopal with the hope of prodding the officials in the Ministry of Education to act speedily on the teaching position at Jabalpur. I had mixed feelings about my year in Agra. On one hand, it had provided me with a buffer between my long years of education and entry into a demanding full-time job. On the other hand, I was disappointed that I had not gained very much on a social, material or professional level. During this period, I had not made any lasting friendships or contacts that I wished to pursue and, materially, I had little money and no additional possessions except for a new pair of woolen trousers, a sports jacket and a cheap tie. Professionally, tinkering with World War II vintage army equipment in what was essentially a large repair shop was hardly a challenging learning experience on which I could build my professional career. The only long-lasting legacy of my year in Agra was the unfortunate habit of smoking, which lasted for a period of more than twenty years. Over the years, I have often wondered if I and members of my immediate family had not been exposed to tobacco smoke, all of us would have enjoyed a more healthy and disease-free life.

Although I was glad that I had spent some time in Agra, exploring its renowned historical sites and relaxing, it left very little lasting impression on me. In some ways, my year's interlude was equivalent to the "gap year" that many fresh university graduates in the developed countries take to travel abroad and see new places, experience different lifestyles and meet new people. As they move through life, the pleasant memories from their travels are tucked away into some corner of their consciousness and when one of these memories comes to the surface, it invokes the pleasant feeling of 'I have been there and done that'. In my case, my fondest memories of Agra are of the breathtaking view of the Taj

Mahal on clear moonlit nights when it glitters like a jewel – especially on the first full moon in autumn after the monsoon rains, and also of the many afternoons I spent reading a book in the shadow of the Taj, while admiring the extraordinary beauty of the monument and the serenity of the surrounding vistas.

CHAPTER 7

Entering the family profession

As I alighted from the train in Bhopal after my overnight journey from Agra, I was fortunate to run into Mr. Bajaj, one of my father's friends from our hometown. Mr. Bajaj was an active member of and a big financial contributor to the ruling Congress Party. Even though he did not hold an elected office, it seems that he wielded considerable influence in the political and administrative corridors of the provincial capital. Mr Bajaj belonged to a family of cloth merchants in our hometown and probably had only a grade school education. However, he was supposed to be quite rich, and it was rumoured that his family had discovered a cache of diamonds in their old house, possibly hidden by a family member of Mr. Dave, the gentleman who was responsible for our community's migration from Gujarat. When Mr Bajaj learned about the purpose of my visit to Bhopal, he invited me to stay with him and assured me that later that day he would accompany me to the Provincial Ministry of Education and introduce me to the appropriate bureaucrat and ask him to expedite the selection process. True to his word, late that morning he walked into the government administration building as if he owned the place, led me to the office of the relevant senior civil servant and apprised him of the purpose of my visit. Mr Bajaj then left to conduct other business and I spent the next hour discussing my qualifications and my interest in the teaching position at the Engineering College with the civil servant. Although he told me that he would follow up on my request with due diligence, I was left with the impression that he was looking for a confirmation from the Principal of the Engineering College about the suitability of my qualifications for the job because the latter was better qualified to make that call..

Satisfied that I had at least started the ball rolling, the next morning I left to spend some time with my family, whom I had not visited for over a year. It was very nice to spend the *Navaratri* and *Dashehra* holidays and enjoy the associated festivities at home with my extended family. Soon after the holiday, I decided to visit the Engineering College at Jabalpur, with a plan of meeting the Principal of the College and to get his endorsement for the teaching position there. In the 1950s, there were very few telephones in India and where they were available; the long distance telephone service was atrocious, requiring hours of waiting times to establish a long distance call. The practice of making a business appointment by phone to meet someone in another city was almost unheard of. The usual practice was to show up without any idea of whether the person you wished to meet was going to be in town or whether he would have time to see you on that day or the next, or if he was even prepared to spare the time to meet you at all. Fortunately the college Principal was in his office on the day I went to meet him. Furthermore, the Administrative Registrar of the College turned out to be an acquaintance from my hometown – his last name was Pandya as well – and he was able to smooth the way for a meeting with the Principal without a long wait. I was advised to wait near the Principal's office until he was ready to see me.

The Principal's office was located on one side of a large open foyer with the College administrative office across it. There was no receptionist or formal reception area except for a couple of old chairs in the foyer. The door to the Principal's office was open, although, like in an old Western movie, a pair of swinging half doors provided some visual privacy. A *peon* or office boy in a shabby khaki uniform sat on a stool beside the door. Every few minutes an electric bell would make a shrill sound and the *peon* would hurry into the office and emerge a few minutes later either to deliver some papers to the administration office or to summon someone for an audience with the Principal. After about half an hour, it was finally my turn and I was ushered into the inner sanctum by the *peon*. The office was very large and was dominated by a solid teak desk which probably measured around 5'x8'. The Principal was seated at the desk in a huge leather chair facing the door. He was a hefty man with a large head and a thick neck, impeccably dressed in a suit and a tie over a white shirt, and exuded an aura of authority. With his large head and prominent jowls, I thought he looked a little bit like Winston Churchill, with the latter's trademark cigar replaced by a pipe. He asked me to take a seat and proceeded to quiz me about my general educational background and on specific technical areas that I had studied during my graduate work. He ended the short meeting by telling me about the breadth and depth of the course and lab work in the electronics and telecommunication department at the College and his own involvement in shaping the program and teaching some of the courses. During our conversation we established that I was an alumnus of the Faculty of Applied Sciences of Calcutta University, his *alma mater* as well – a fact which gained some additional empathy from him. This fact also allowed him to quickly assess my academic background and suitability for teaching the relevant undergraduate and graduate courses at his institution. After the meeting, I was quite confident that I had made a good impression and left for home with a feeling that he would provide favourable input to the Ministry of Education.

However, as they say "the show isn't over until the fat lady sings". Thus my ordeal with the bureaucracy would only end when I had a firm job offer from the Ministry of Education. In two weeks, I was back in Bhopal knocking on doors at various levels of the administration, deploying whatever limited influence I could muster as a rookie in the fine art of navigating entrenched bureaucratic channels. Finally, after three days of intense canvassing, I had the desired piece of paper saying that I had been appointed as an Assistant Professor in the Electronics and Telecommunications department at the Government Engineering College, Jabalpur, with a monthly salary of 250 Indian Rupees with an addition 40 Rupees per month as Dearness Allowance (D.A.). At the exchange rate in 1957, the salary probably amounted to about $100 a month. I left for Jabalpur the same night and officially joined the teaching staff of the Engineering College the next day, following in the footsteps of my grandfather, my father, and three of my siblings who had been or currently were in the teaching profession.

Life as an employed bachelor

The Engineering College campus is located about five kilometres from the Jabalpur city centre, on the eastern outskirts, with a small lake at the back which is surrounded by low, bare hills on the far side. The east-west provincial highway connecting Jabalpur to the outlying towns intersects the campus, dividing it into two distinct parts. All the buildings housing the various teaching, lab and sports facilities are located on the north side of the highway and the staff and student residential facilities are located on the south side. The highway also leads to a very large ammunition or ordinance factory that belongs to the Defence Ministry. It employed thousands of workers, the majority of whom commuted by bicycles from the city. This meant that on weekdays, the one-lane highway became a sea of bicycles from seven to eight in the morning and from five to six in the evening, essentially closing the road to any other traffic. The campus was built around the former Robertson College, an arts and science institution established during the British Raj, around 1905. The graceful, old colonial building of Robertson College is still used by one of the engineering faculties, but it is now surrounded by new concrete structures, so that the building and the lake behind it are no longer visible from the main road. As is traditional in most institutions of higher learning in India, the College provided residential facilities within easy walking distance not only for the students but also for the teaching and support staff at a nominal rent. The College owned various types of houses on the campus. There were 'English professors' bungalows and 'Indian professors' bungalows which originally belonged to Robertson College and were allotted to higher ranking teaching staff. These were quite spacious houses, circa 1905. The main difference between the two was that in the 'English professors' bungalows, the kitchen was located some distance from the main house and the toilets located inside, while it was just the reverse in the 'Indian professors' accommodation. In addition to these bungalows, the College also owned a large number of smaller but relatively newer houses (circa 1950) to accommodate different categories of college employees.

Fortunately, one of the newer bungalows designated for my rank in the pecking order was currently empty and available to me. The bungalow was one of a number of identical houses and was situated next to the boundary wall of the residential campus. When I inspected it, my initial thought was that the architect who designed these houses either had little imagination or had spent all of his professional life designing army barracks. The bungalow consisted of three equal-sized rooms in a row, opening on to a lattice-covered veranda in the front and an open veranda at the back, with a bathroom and kitchen on opposite ends of the back veranda. The back veranda looked out on to an enclosed private courtyard with a typical Asian style 'squat and pee' WC located in one corner and a large *Raat ki Rani* (Queen of the Night) bush in the other, whose flowers released a strong sweet fragrance at night. The house came with two 'servants' quarters', located a few yards behind the main house, to provide accommodation for personal servants. In spite of the unimaginative layout, I was thrilled because for the first time in my adult life, I had a whole house to myself with more space than I could possibly use as a single person with few earthly possessions.

During the current and the last visit to Jabalpur, I had been bunking with an old friend and classmate from Raipur who was finishing his last year of engineering studies and was living in the student residence. Since the house I was to move into was unfurnished and unequipped for cooking and other daily necessities, my friend helped me rent some basic furniture and buy minimal kitchen and household supplies. I also arranged to have one of the students' dining halls supply morning and evening meals to my house. I hired a part-time servant-boy to fetch the meals from the residence, prepare my morning and afternoon tea and do the basic house cleaning. With these domestic arrangements in place, I moved into my bungalow and joined the academic community with a great deal of pride and a sense that I was at the start of a journey that would be personally interesting and professionally satisfying.

Since the academic session was already in progress, I did not have much time to get my bearings before I had to start teaching. Based on my academic background, I was asked to teach a couple of advanced courses to graduate students, which for a rooky lecturer like me, meant a lot of hours spent in preparing for the lectures. However, I found that I was enjoying the work and was generally pleased that I could establish a good rapport with the students and effectively communicate complex technical concepts. Within a short period of time, I felt quite comfortable in the academic environment – so much so that when I received two additional offers for jobs with the Central Government as a result of my earlier interviews in Delhi and Simla, after some hesitation I decided to decline them despite the popular view that these government positions would likely offer better pay and brighter career prospects. I believe that this represented a significant decision for me, and, in retrospect, I think I chose the right path at this critical crossroad.

While I was fairly busy trying to keep pace with my teaching responsibilities, I was also gradually finding my way in the social and political landscape that influenced the College staff members. I soon discovered that, for the employees and their families living in the College housing, there were very limited opportunities for extracurricular activities. The College did not provide any facilities for staff members to pursue personal interests in arts, entertainment or sports. The city, where such facilities could be found, was a long distance away and most residents of the staff colony did not have access to transportation. Whenever I wanted to see a movie or meet my friends at a coffee house in the city, I had to pedal five kilometres each way on a rented bicycle. Since the community was isolated with few outlets for escaping the closed atmosphere, the main source of entertainment –especially for those living in the College staff colony – tended to be gossiping about the professional and personal lives of their colleagues. The prevailing authoritative and at times patronizing management style further contributed to the spread of gossip, rumours and professional rivalries. This was my first real job and I had little experience in the work-place environment that frequently exists in academic institutions. I was therefore ill-prepared to navigate in it. Fortunately, not too long after I joined the teaching staff at the College there was a change in management which was less authoritative and opaque so that for the most part, I was spared from having to deal with the unhealthy and unfamiliar politics that I had originally landed into

During the first six months, my teaching responsibilities kept me very busy and I had little time for any extracurricular activities, except for the odd bicycle trip to the Empire theatre which showed English language movies or to have a friendly game of badminton with my teaching colleagues. It was a relief when the academic year ended in May and the two-month summer vacation began. Unlike Western countries, where people plan travel and relaxation for their vacations, in those days few people in India had enough disposable income to afford such indulgences. Most people spent their vacation time visiting family and friends. I was not keen to spend two months with my family in my hometown, where my circle of friends had greatly depleted over the years. However, I had little choice in the matter for the simple reason that during these two months the student residences and their dining halls were closed, effectively cutting off my daily supply of meals. At this time, I did not have a full-time cook to prepare meals and it was too far to bike down to the restaurants in the city twice a day in the intense summer heat. So, in spite of the fact that I had a job and a house in Jabalpur, I spent the summer vacation with my family in Hatta. This turned out to be the last long summer that I would spend with my parents and siblings at home. My future visits home were generally short, lasting for a week or ten days at the most, and took place during important holidays like *Diwali* or for special occasions like family weddings.

The next academic year started in July, soon after the arrival of the monsoon rains. After my return from the summer vacation, I was fortunate to find an excellent cook who was efficient, reliable and honest, who took over the duties of setting up the kitchen, doing the grocery shopping, and preparing morning and evening tea, as well as the daily meals. Sujan Singh, or Pandit as we called him, was also employed as a *peon* at the college and he supplemented his income with the salary and meals he earned as a cook. In addition to Pandit, a maid servant came in to wash the dishes and do general house cleaning. A third servant came every morning to clean the bathroom and the toilet. The prevailing Indian caste system required that these three different household tasks be assigned to persons of the proper caste. Besides these daily servants, I also had to retain a *Dhobi* who came every week to pick up laundry and a barber who came every few weeks to cut my hair.

With these arrangements in place, I was all set for a comfortable bachelor's life. However, with all its amenities, as well as spare space, my home soon became more like a guest house than a private residence. During the four years that I lived in that house, there were very few extended periods when some friend, friend of a friend, or a near or distant relative was not staying with me as a house guest. One of the houseguests was a senior colleague in my department who had just returned from the United States after completing his Doctoral studies at the University of Illinois. He stayed with me for over a month while awaiting accommodation and encouraged and motivated me to explore opportunities for further studies abroad.

I quickly settled into my teaching responsibilities and integrated well into the campus life. I made a few close friendships among the College staff as well as outside the campus, and frequently met them at the India Coffee House in the city for an evening of camaraderie or at some bachelor pad to play a few rubbers of bridge. However, plans were already afoot to bring my carefree bachelor days to an end. Given that I had a steady job with reasonable future prospects and that my thirtieth birthday was not far off, my parents were following the age-old Indian tradition of arranged marriages and searching for a bride who, in their opinion, would be suitable for me. Towards the end of 1960, my father informed me that they had lined up a prospective bride. She lived with her family in Jabalpur and was studying home economics at the local women's college. Her grandparents were residents of my hometown and I knew them and many of her relatives. I met her family briefly when I saw her for the first time. She was an average-looking woman with a college education, who came from a respectable Gujarati Brahmin family which was well known to my family, and whose horoscope seemed to match mine. These were sufficient grounds for my parents to declare that the match was suitable and I soon found myself engaged to be married at some yet-to-be-determined date in the near future. After our formal engagement, I had little contact with my prospective bride, even though we lived only a few miles apart, which was normal in terms of the social customs of the time.

As it turned out, the question of setting a date for the wedding never arose because soon after the engagement I learned that I was likely to go to Canada for further studies in the fall of 1961, and I had no intention of getting married before I went abroad. In the late summer of 1961, the Canadian High Commission informed me that I had been accepted for graduate studies at the University of Toronto, under an exchange program between Commonwealth countries whereby engineers and scientists from developing countries could enrol in postgraduate programmes in countries like U.K., Canada and Australia. For reasons I have mentioned earlier, I opted for the University of Toronto in Canada. I was advised to present myself at the Canadian High Commission in Delhi to complete the formalities for a students' Visa. After returning from Delhi with all the necessary formalities completed, all I had to do was to wait for word that my flight to Toronto has been confirmed with a firm departure date. I spent the waiting period getting ready for the trip and life in Canada. This essentially consisted of getting rid of my meagre household items, visiting my home to say goodbye to my parents and siblings, and adding a few warm clothes to my modest wardrobe, including my first-ever suit.

In early September I received my final marching orders from the Canadian High Commission and left for Delhi to catch my BOAC flight to London en route to Toronto. I spent a few days in Delhi staying with Mani, my friend from Calcutta, who had accepted a job with the Civil Aviation Authority in Delhi and lived in a government hostel. After doing some last-minute shopping, I caught my outbound flight from the rather shabby Palam Airport in Delhi and as the BOAC turbo jet lifted to the sky and made a slow turn to the west, little did I know that with that westward turn, my future was taking a similar turn.

INDIA (1964 – 1968)

****

CHAPTER 8

Preparing to launch in uncharted waters

The QUANTAS flight which was the last leg of my journey back from Canada landed early in the morning at Delhi's Palam Airport which was covered in a soupy fog. After spending almost two hours creeping through immigration control, baggage collection, and the customs line-ups, I finally emerged from the terminal and was immediately swallowed up by a frenzied mass of people – some there to receive relatives and friends, others to sell goods and services to incoming passengers. After living in Canada where things are well organized, people are extremely polite, and public spaces are clean and well maintained, it was disconcerting to suddenly encounter the chaotic atmosphere, shabby public spaces, dirty facilities and uncaring service providers such as: public servants, shopkeepers, and taxi drivers. Rather than indulging in nostalgia for what I had just left behind, I made a conscious effort to overcome my reverse culture shock, and quickly adjusted to the situation. After haggling with one of Delhi's taxi drivers who are notorious for their dishonesty and rudeness, I made my way to the Janapath Hotel near Connaught Circus. The hotel was owned and operated by the Department of Tourism of the Indian Government and provided questionable service and substandard cleanliness. Because of the overnight stops in London and Dubai, I was not particularly jet lagged, and decided to have a quick shower and breakfast before stepping out on Janapath, a busy thoroughfare lined with colonial-era Government buildings, including the Central Post and Telegraph complex. I used the telegraph facilities at the complex to send a few telegrams to tell people that I had arrived safely in Delhi, including one to my father letting him know that I planned to be home within a few days

Getting family's blessing and support

After spending another day in Delhi visiting with my friends Mani and Mehta, I took a train to Jabalpur with the intention of resuming my teaching work at the Engineering College. A friend and fellow teacher at the College was kind enough to invite me to stay with him. He belonged to a large family of seven brothers and three sisters, most of them lived with their parents in a spacious house near the city centre. The next morning my host informed me that some visitors were waiting to see me. When I entered the living room, I was surprised and disconcerted to find that the visitors were none other than the parents of the girl to whom I was engaged to before leaving for Canada. After I met Margaret and started considering the possibility of a more permanent relationship with her, I had written to the girl's parents and indicated that there was a fair chance that the engagement might not follow its normal path ultimately culminating in a wedding.. However, I was ill prepared to face them so soon after landing in India and felt awkward and guilty for having placed them in such a painful situation. In our community, a broken engagement was a very rare occurrence, and often reflected badly on the girl and, to a lesser extent, on her family. I do not recall the details of this difficult conversation, but at the end of it they reluctantly accepted, although with obvious anger and resentment, that a return to the original plan was not a likely possibility.

This unexpected encounter made it even more urgent for me to discuss the matter with my father and family and seek their approval and support for marrying the girl I had fallen in love with in Canada. The next morning, I boarded an early bus and headed to my hometown to visit with my family. I had been away for more than two years, during which time my mother had passed away and one of my brothers had got married and become a father of a beautiful daughter. The most pressing objective of the visit was to inform them of my intentions and alleviate their concerns about a venture that could be considered completely unorthodox and beyond the comprehension of my family and community. The girl I wished to marry was not only from a different country, but also was from a race, culture, caste, community, religion, and upbringing of which my family had little knowledge and no understanding. Their perception of Western culture was entirely based on sketchy accounts from books or magazines about the ways of the British ruling class in India, which hardly reflected the true essence of Western culture or its fundamental values.

In my discussions with my father, rather than dwelling on the broader issues and differences between Eastern and Western cultures, I focused on Margaret's specific attributes and attitudes that would enable her to rapidly integrate into our culture and way of life, provided our family and friends were prepared to give her a fair chance. I emphasized the fact that Margaret's upbringing was not that different from my own, in that she was raised in a loving and caring family in a small town, with many of her relatives living in close proximity. I also talked about her generosity of spirit, her love for children, her caring nature, her interest in and interaction with other cultures as part of her work and travels, and her rational and pragmatic, rather than dogmatic world view.

In a sense I was trying to re-create, though in a limited way and in a different context, the story of the first ship load of Zoroastrian or Parsee refugees who arrived on the West coast of India from Persia somewhere between the eighth and tenth century CE. The story goes that the Zoroastrian leader found that the local ruler was reluctant to accept these people from a distant country, who practised a strange religion, spoke a foreign language, and belonged to a different ethnicity and unfamiliar culture. In order to assuage the ruler's fear of the unfamiliar and the unknown, the leader asked for a glass of fresh, unsweetened milk. The leader then added a few drops of honey to the milk and asked the ruler to taste the milk. He then explained that, just as the addition of a small amount of honey had enriched the taste and nutritional quality of the milk without in any way degrading its overall appearance and its quality, he assured the ruler that his people would not only assimilate quickly and completely, but would also enrich and enhance the overall social, cultural and economic life of the land. The rest is history. The Parsees now form an important component of the diverse and colourful mosaic of Indian society and continue to be very significant contributors to the social, cultural and economic life of the country.

My approach was perhaps not as elegant or as intuitive as that of the Zoroastrian leader, but ultimately I was able to convince my father, the patriarch of our family, that in spite of the apparent dissimilarities between our cultures and backgrounds, welcoming Margaret into the family would not only make me very happy, but would also be a positive and enriching experience for the entire family. Our story also had an interesting and completely coincidental corollary to the Zoroastrian tale. In our community, when a bride comes into the family, she is given a new first name, and strangely the name my father chose for Margaret was *Madhuri* which means 'one who is (sweet) like honey'. To this day, members of my side of the family always address her as *Madhuri*.

Preparing for the wedding and after

Once my father had given his consent, I was confident that as the patriarch of the family he would make sure that the rest of the family would make every effort to welcome Margaret and treat her with the love and respect a daughter-in-law deserved. Glad to have accomplished the most urgent and challenging objective of my visit home, I once again travelled to Bhopal, the provincial capital, to chase the bureaucrats and obtain the piece of paper which I needed to resume my teaching job at the Engineering College. Having finally obtained the necessary documentation, I arrived in Jabalpur in early January in 1964 and started to put my professional and personal life back in some order. I was hoping to move into one of the staff residences and establish a household with the help of Pandit, my former cook and household manager, who was still around. Unfortunately, no staff residences were immediately available and I ended up sharing a small residence with a colleague who was currently leading a bachelor's existence because, as is customary in many Indian families, his young, pregnant wife, had gone home to her parents until their baby was born. The wife's family was quite rich and had given him a new motor scooter as part of the dowry, and most evenings we would ride the scooter into town to meet with a group of friends at the India Coffee House, or on weekends to have a few shots of cheap army rum and play bridge until late at night

The arrangement came to an end in early May when the summer vacation started and the student residences closed down and we could no more depend on their kitchen to deliver our daily meals. My colleague was going home to be with his wife and the newborn child and rather than going to my ancestral home, I decided to move into the local YMCA hostel. It was located in a nice part of town not too far from the India Coffee House and the bachelor pad where our group of friends tended to congregate. The hostel was an old sprawling bungalow from the British era, built on a large piece of land with wide verandas. The bungalow was cut up into a number of one-room units with a central dining hall and common meeting area. My unit consisted of a narrow, stuffy room with basic furniture, a bathroom and a small covered porch fronting on a large open space where I moved my bed to sleep under the open sky during the hot summer nights. The monthly rent included three daily meals served in the dining hall and morning and afternoon tea delivered to the room. I was quite happy with the arrangement and spent the hottest part of the summer days indoors reading books, and the relatively cooler evenings with my friends at the Coffee House or the movies.

The stay at the YMCA came to an end when I was informed that I had been selected, along with my friend and colleague, Robi Dasgupta, to attend a four-week educational seminar for technical teachers from all over India. The venue was the Engineering College in the city of Pune in western India, located about 200 km south of Bombay. The seminar was funded and organized by the United States Technical Cooperation Mission which also provided most of the American instructors. I looked forward to spending four weeks in Pune which is considered to be an important cultural and industrial city and also has a more temperate climate than Jabalpur. Robi and I were billeted in a students' residence and spent most of our free time exploring the city. The unexpected death of our first Prime Minister Jawahar Lal Nehru occurred during our stay in Pune. For three days, the city and the country came to a standstill to mourn the death of a visionary leader who had been a stalwart in India's struggle for independence and had firmly put the newly independent nation on the path of democracy and secularism.

The educational seminar, unfortunately, was not well organized and did not have sufficient focus on the specific issues facing technical education in India. However, I was glad to have spent these weeks with my friend Robi, with whom I could discuss the challenges which I faced in the coming months. Although my family had given me their blessing to marry Margaret, without knowing her, her family, or her culture, they had left the details of 'when', 'where' and 'how' the actual ceremony would take place entirely in my hands. I needed all the advice and support I could muster from my close friends and colleagues to put together a plan and ensure that it would be successful. Since Robi came from a well-established Bengali family in Jabalpur and had many friends and contacts in the city, he was a good person to guide me through the practical details. Considering the time needed for me to plan the big event and for Margaret to wind up her affairs, bid good bye to her folks, and schedule her travel, as well as the fact that a staff residence would not be available before July, I decided on a mid-October wedding date and advised Margaret accordingly. The cooler weather began in northern India in October, and it was also the month of *Dashehra* and *Diwali*, two very important Hindu festivals, when family members generally get together. I felt that this festive period would be a suitable time to introduce Margaret to the family and begin the mutual familiarization process. I had less than four months to arrange everything, not just for her arrival and the wedding, but also the practical details of our life together in a society and culture which would be at best, unfamiliar, if not totally alien, to her.

Having resolved the question of the timing for the wedding, I still had to decide on what type of ceremony would be appropriate, given the differences in our religious backgrounds, and select a suitable venue for the ceremony. It was clear that the wedding had to take place in Jabalpur where I could count on my friends and colleagues for help and support in facilitating the practical arrangements. To my knowledge, our inter-racial, inter-faith, and international wedding was the first of its kind to be held in the city of Jabalpur and there was no precedent to guide me. The three obvious options were a Civil, a Christian or a Hindu ceremony. In the case of inter faith weddings, some religions require that the partner from outside the faith convert to the other partner's faith. In Hinduism, there does not seem to be any such requirement and it is generally up to the individual partners how they conduct their spiritual lives. This does not mean that Hinduism prohibits people from other religious backgrounds from entering and practicing the faith. In the past, Hinduism did spread outside India, especially in Southeast Asia. The temples of Angkor Wat in Cambodia and the mainly Hindu population of Bali attest to this missionary spirit in distant past. Generally most conversions to Hinduism are the result of individual inclinations rather than an active missionary campaign or proselytizing, and most often do not involve a formal 'conversion' ritual like a Christian baptism– one only needs to adopt the 'Hindu way of life' to practice the religion.

Given Hinduism's rather inclusive and non-dogmatic approach, I felt that if Margaret had no serious reservations, a ceremony based on Hindu traditions would be the best choice. Another advantage of a Hindu ceremony would be its familiarity to my family which would give them an opportunity to take greater part in the ceremony and welcome the new bride into the family fold. Having made this decision, I still had many more hurdles to cross. The Hindu wedding ceremonies which I had attended in the past were lengthy and arduous affairs, lasting as long as three days, with many peripheral rituals surrounding the main event. As well, the Hindu wedding ceremony generally takes place at the bride's residence with the groom's party, called the *Baraat*, hosted by the bride's parents for the duration. Such a lengthy and elaborate event was not practical. I therefore had to find a shorter version of the ceremony which would include the essential rituals associated with a Hindu wedding, and find a suitable place to hold the event and a Hindu priest to conduct it. Fortunately, I happened to mention these challenges to Professor Deshpande, a senior colleague who had come to know Margaret during his short visit to Toronto. Professor Deshpande was a member of the Maharashtrian Brahmin community which, like the Gujratis, came from the western part of India, and the wedding rituals of the two communities were quite similar. With the help of his family priest, he not only offered to arrange for a shorter version of the ceremony (about three hours instead of three days), but also offered his large bungalow as the venue for the event. In addition, he offered to adopt Margaret as his daughter so that he could 'give away the bride' which is an essential part of the ceremony.

While working on the wedding arrangements, I was also making preparations for our life after the wedding. Practical items such as a suitable house, furniture, servants, and various other aspects of day-to-day living as a family in India also needed to be organized. In July, I was allocated one of the staff residences on the college campus. The house was essentially a replica of the unit that I had occupied before leaving for Canada, with the two bungalows practically facing one another across a large open space. Fortunately, Pandit, my former cook, was available and accepted my offer to become our permanent cook and agreed to set up the kitchen and run the household, including hiring additional part-time help to take care of the daily cleaning chores. As soon as I moved into the assigned residence, I started to scope out the essential furnishings and amenities that would make life a bit easier for Margaret who was used to living in Canada, with Western facilities and many labour-saving devices. It was not possible to replicate the facilities of a Canadian household in a small city in India, but I was able to upgrade the bathroom, installing a sink and a shower. I also had a large sink and Western-style counter with a two-ring gas burner installed in the kitchen. However, there was no practical way of replacing the Asian style 'squat and pee' water closet located in the corner of our enclosed courtyard with a Western commode. I was counting on the fact that Margaret had already been exposed to such facilities during her back-packing travels through Europe in the late 1950s.

In consultation with Professor Deshpande and my family, we decided that the afternoon of October 18th would be the most suitable date for the wedding. While I was busy making practical arrangements, such as sending out invitations, deciding on the menu for the wedding dinner, and booking our honeymoon trip, Margaret was busy getting ready for the long journey to a new country and an unfamiliar culture, and bidding goodbye to her family and friends, with little prospect of returning in the foreseeable future. As she prepared to board the ship for her ocean journey, I wonder if she thought about her pioneer forefathers who embarked on their voyages to Canada from Ireland and Scotland, facing an uncertain future and with little hope of ever seeing their homeland again. In retrospect, I admire her courage, her faith, and the depth of her love that prompted her to part from her family and friends and her comfortable life in Canada to travel halfway around the world to a new country to live among people who practiced a different religion with different gods. After all, she had only known me for little more than six months. I recall that in one of her letters, Margaret whose middle name is Ruth, invoked the story of Ruth from the Old Testament. According to the biblical story, Ruth goes with her mother-in-law, Naomi, who is returning to Bethlehem from the land of Moab after her husband's death. Ruth, a Moabite and a widow herself, declares *"Where you go, I will go and where you lodge, I will lodge, your people shall be my people, and your God my God"*.

Margaret arrives in India

Margaret had decided to travel to India by ship rather than take an aeroplane because the long and leisurely ocean voyage would give her an opportunity to get over the sadness of leaving her life and loved ones in Canada and also to mentally prepare her for the new experiences awaiting her at the journey's end. She sailed in mid-September from Montreal where her cousin and his wife, with whom I had stayed before leaving Canada in January, wished her *bon voyage*. After spending a few days with one of her friends in England, she boarded the P&O ship that was scheduled to dock in Bombay on October 13th, 1964. Unfortunately, due to some archaic bureaucratic rules, I could not get away from my work in time to travel to Bombay and meet her when she arrived. However, two of my cousins were living in Bombay at the time and at my request, they agreed to meet and greet Margaret when she disembarked. One cousin and her husband were teachers at the University and the other cousin held a senior position in the railways which entitled him to a large bungalow in the suburbs of Bombay, along with a score of servants. They met Margaret as the ship docked in Bombay and, though she had reservations at the Taj hotel, my cousin who lived in the suburbs insisted that she be their guest for the duration of her stay. It was very fortunate that Margaret was not only able to meet my family on her arrival, but was also able to observe, first hand, the lifestyle of a middle-class Indian family. She received her first lessons in eating Indian food with her fingers, and learned how to properly drape a *sari* consisting of six yards of material. Along with my cousins she went out to buy a wedding *sari* and learned to navigate through a crowded Indian bazaar. I am sure she was overwhelmed by the crowded streets of Bombay, with their varied and chaotic traffic, ubiquitous beggars on the streets and blood-like stains on the sidewalks caused by people spitting *paan* juice. I was glad that, in my absence, the hospitality and guidance provided by my cousins in Bombay greatly helped her to overcome her culture shock and eased her way into this new country and unfamiliar social environment.

On the afternoon of October 14th, I finally arrived in Bombay, accompanied by my uncle with whom I had stayed during my high school and undergraduate years in Raipur. My father had asked him to be there as a senior representative of our family to welcome Margaret and assure her that, regardless of the differences in race, religion, and nationality, she would be afforded all the respect and affection due to a new bride entering the family. As I got off the train in Bombay, I saw Margaret, together with my cousin and his family waiting on the platform. She was dressed in a *sari* and was carrying a bouquet of flowers which she handed to me as we met. Then she reached down and touched my uncle's feet – a common Indian gesture of respect for elders which she must have recently learned from my cousins. Even though we had been separated for more than ten months, hugging and kissing each other in public – especially in the presence of my family members – were a definite 'no no'. A quick handshake and the exchange of the bouquet of flowers was the best we could do. We all took a local commuter train to my cousin's large residence where we were to spend the next couple of nights before leaving for Jabalpur for the wedding ceremony. Fortunately, my cousin and especially his wife were sympathetic to our need for privacy after such a long period of separation, and they put the two of us in the same bedroom, for which we were very grateful. Over dinner, Margaret recounted her first impressions of Bombay, her experiences with Indian Customs and Immigration and her time spent with my cousins shopping for her wedding *sari* – a typical red silk wedding *sari* which she still wears on special occasions, including our wedding anniversaries.

Finally, it was bedtime and as we retired to our bedroom I felt that we should at least be formally engaged, if not married, before sharing a bedroom. I formally (and unconditionally) proposed and gave her the engagement ring, an unusual design consisting of a coiled cobra with a diamond on its crown and two rubies for its eyes. The ring was part of several custom-made, 22 karat gold jewellery items (rings, bracelets, necklace, ear rings, etc.) that my father had sent as gifts for Margaret to welcome her as a daughter-in-law. Wearing a red silk *sari* and pure gold jewellery is *de rigueur* for a middle-class Indian bride. Margaret and I spent most of next day with my other cousin and her husband. This particular cousin was close to my age, and while growing up, we had spent a lot of time together when her family visited us during the summers. We spent the day shopping and went to the beach for a swim in the Arabian Sea. The next afternoon Margaret, my uncle and I boarded the train for Jabalpur at Bombay's famous Victoria Terminus or VT. We said goodbye to my cousins who had come to see us off with loads of food for our overnight journey

The Hindu wedding

We arrived in Jabalpur in the early afternoon the day before our wedding and were greeted by Professor and Mrs Deshpande and a number of my friends and colleagues. Professor Deshpande drove us to his home where Margaret was to spend the night in their guest room. Some of my family members, including my uncle's family, had already arrived and the rest were scheduled to arrive the next day. I had arranged for them to stay at another bungalow nearby which was also the venue of the wedding dinner. After Margaret had freshened up, we walked over to meet members of my family who had come to attend the wedding. Afterwards, I showed her the small bungalow that would be our home as a married couple. That evening, my friend, with whom I had briefly stayed on my return from Canada, drove us to the city to do some last-minute shopping for items required for the wedding ceremony. We decided to call it an early night because the next day was going to be a very busy one for both of us. I had to make sure that all the necessary arrangements for the ceremony and the wedding dinner were in place and also look after the needs of my family members who had come for the wedding. Professor Deshpande and his family had kindly agreed to take on all the roles and responsibilities of an Indian bride's family, including the practical arrangements for the various wedding rituals, and preparing the bride for the ceremony. This generally includes a ritual turmeric bath and decorative painting of hands and feet with *henna*, followed by donning the wedding *sari*, the appropriate jewellery, and a tiara made of flowers. The ladies and little girls from the staff colony were very excited to meet the 'foreign' bride, and were a great help to the Deshpandes in all the preparations.

The wedding ceremony started in the late afternoon with the formal arrival and welcoming of the groom, accompanied by family and friends, at the bride's residence, and lasted for about three hours. Hindu weddings are elaborate affairs with many rituals to symbolize various aspects of a man and a woman committing themselves to each other for life, including how they should conduct themselves as a married couple, and the roles and responsibilities of the family towards the new member of the extended family. For example, the father of the bride puts the bride's hand into the groom's, symbolizing that the bride's family is offering their daughter to the groom in marriage, and the bride and groom feed each other rice cooked over the sacred fire, symbolizing their mutual love and affection. In the naming ritual, the bride is given a new name chosen by the groom's family to indicate that the bride is now a full member of the groom's family. Of course, since India is a large and culturally very diverse country, within a Hindu wedding the rituals can vary between different regions and between different communities within a region.

Unlike a Western wedding where the priest or minister has the authority from the State to marry a couple, in a Hindu wedding, the bride and groom marry each other by jointly making very specific and detailed vows prescribed by the scriptures and traditions. The sacred fire, God in heaven and the invited guests bear witness to this process that culminates in marriage. Once the couple has taken the necessary vows in the prescribed manner, in the presence of these witnesses, they are considered legally married. The role of the Hindu priest is to oversee the proper conduct of the wedding rituals and mainly consists of reciting appropriate Sanskrit verses and guiding the couple and their family members through the various rituals.

The wedding vows fall into two broad categories. In the first category, the four vows are general in nature and bind the couple to conduct their lives according to the four basic goals of Hindu way of life, which are:

Dharma: leading a righteous life;
Artha: prosperity with respect to material goods and comfort;

Kama: energy and passion in the enjoyment of physical pleasures: and

Moksha: liberation from the cycle of birth and death through self-realization.

In the second category, the seven vows relate to more specific commitments for the conduct of married life, and include:

Let us provide for our household, stay in good health and carry out our duties and responsibilities to each other, and our families

Let us develop our mental and spiritual powers;

Let us increase our wealth and comfort by righteous and proper means

Let us acquire knowledge, happiness and harmony by mutual love, respect and trust;

Let us be blessed with a contended family of strong, virtuous and heroic children;

Let us be blessed with long lives; and

Let us remain true companions, committed only to each other

The bride and groom take each of these seven vows, as they circle the sacred fire seven times, while they are literally tied together with one end of the bride's *sari* tied to one end of the shawl worn by the groom. Since very few people in India can speak Sanskrit (just as very few people speak Latin in the West), the actual vows, originally written in Sanskrit, are enunciated by the priest and the couple is only required to affirm their consent. After we had taken our vows and completed the rituals in the bride's house, we were accompanied by my family and friends to the groom's residence, the house where my family was temporarily lodged. There, we completed a few more rituals, such as 'naming the bride' in which Margaret was formally given the name *Madhuri* by my family, and the ritual in which the couple seeks the blessing of the elders in the family by touching their feet. The rituals were followed by an Indian wedding dinner which consisted of purely vegetarian fare, prepared in-house by our cook with the assistance of some temporary help. It was almost 11:00 pm by the time we said goodnight to all of the dinner guests and family and returned to our own little bungalow as a married couple. We were surprised to see that our friends had decorated our bedroom with loads of flowers and the room was filled with the fragrance of marigolds and roses. It had been an exciting, although a long, day for both of us and after a brief toast of Indian-made brandy (champagne was pretty much unheard of in India in those days) we prepared for our first night together as husband and wife. When we were unexpectedly woken up at 3.00

am by the alarm clock we realized that our friends had done a bit more than decorating the bedroom with flowers.

It had been more than ten months since we had said good bye at the Montreal airport in January to this night, and we had faced many uncertainties, misgivings, and challenges to reach this milestone. There had been times when I felt apprehensive and discouraged about our venture into this uncharted territory, but there had also been times when I felt hopeful and optimistic that, given the unconditional acceptance and support of our two families and encouragement of our friends, we would overcome the challenges. However, as they say, getting married is the easy part – although it had not been that easy for us. Sustaining our love, affection and loyalty, while we faced the inevitable ups and downs that the future would hold, would be the real test. In our case, coming from the opposite sides of the world, both geographically and culturally, it was especially hard to anticipate the kind of challenges that lay ahead. We had just launched our canoe into uncharted waters and were getting ready to navigate through unknown twists and turns in the path ahead, drawing comfort and encouragement from the fact that our families and friends were reassuring us from the shores that they were prepared to give us a helping hand, if we needed to *portage* around unusually rough waters.

CHAPTER 9

The journey begins – West meets East

Honeymoon in the Himalayas

We spent the next day bidding goodbye to the members of my family and friends who had come for the wedding from out of town. In the evening some of my bachelor friends had arranged a dinner party at a local hotel. On this occasion Margaret experienced the novelty of being addressed as Mrs Pandya; she also tasted beer for the first time – breaking a promise made to her mother never to indulge in beer drinking at the risk of becoming like one of the drunken old ladies often seen staggering out of the local pub in her hometown. Next day we left by train on our honeymoon trip with the first stop being a visit to the Taj Mahal – a symbol of beauty, love and loyalty. We stayed at a small hotel in the old part of Agra and, in the morning, hired a *Tonga* to visit the Taj Mahal and a number of other *Mugal* era architectural monuments around the city. We spent a few hours admiring the intricacies of the extensive inlay work in and around the central marble structure as well as that of the marble lattice screen surrounding the resting places of empress Mumtaj Mahal and her husband *Mugal* emperor Shah Jahan. We came back in the early night to enjoy the stunning view of the Taj in the light of an almost full moon on a clear night. It is a unique and unforgettable experience: one can sit for hours in the beautifully laid out garden and not tire of staring at the Taj awash in moonlight, gleaming like a jewel.

After our brief visit to Agra to see the Taj Mahal, we caught an overnight train to a place called Kathgodaam in the foothills of the Himalayas. There we boarded a bus to take us to Nainital, a hill station and holiday resort located around a mountain lake in the Himalayan foothills. Nainital is part of an area called Kumaon in the lower Himalayas made famous by the British big game hunter and author Jim Corbett who wrote about his adventures in big game hunting in this area during the British Raj. One of his better known books called The Man Eaters of Kumaon was a text book in my school days. The conservation area in Kumaon is named Jim Corbett Park, after him. The road to Nainital was a single lane strip, with innumerable switch backs, climbing over 6,000 feet. The combination of the narrow road hugging the mountains on one side and a sheer drop on the other with hairpin switchbacks every few minutes, along with the generally spotty maintenance record of government-run buses in India, made for a journey that was less than relaxing. We were glad to arrive safely at the bus terminal in Nainital. However, our first view of the beautiful blue green waters of the pear shaped lake and the soaring mountains surrounding it, was more than adequate compensation for the tense trip.

As soon as we disembarked from the bus, we were accosted by a throng of agents from local hotels and guest houses, including one from the YMCA, all promoting their respective establishments. We decided to stay at the YMCA because one of my acquaintances in Jabalpur had told me that his sister was the manager of the Nainital YMCA. We walked the short distance to the YMCA, accompanied by the agent and a porter carrying our luggage. The YMCA was a single story, stone building abutting a hill at the back and a wide open veranda in the front. There were about twenty rooms opening off the wide arched veranda. The veranda looked out on the front terrace and the garden which was surrounded by a low stone wall and overlooked the lake below. The facilities were well maintained and the room rental included three meals a day, as well as morning and afternoon tea which was delivered to our room. Looking back, perhaps we would have appreciated a double bed instead of the two single beds, but since we were on our honeymoon and the nights were cooler in the mountains we were happy to snuggle in one of the beds until the bearer knocked on the door in early morning to announce the arrival of our so called 'bed tea'. All in all, with the glorious view of the spacious garden, the mountain lake and the Himalayas, we were very happy with the choice of our honeymoon retreat.

Our week in Nainital passed quickly, with days spent exploring the winding streets of the town, savouring street food and visiting nearby places of interest. We would have liked to have stayed longer, but the mid-term college vacation for *Diwali* was soon coming to an end and I wanted us to celebrate the important festival of *Diwali* at my ancestral home so that Margaret could meet my extended family in its normal habitat. Therefore we bid a reluctant goodbye to Nainital and made our way to Delhi to spend a brief time with my friend Mani, who had also recently got married and now lived in a small one bedroom flat in a Delhi suburb. After visiting Mani, our next stop was Jhansi, an important railway town and a place made famous by Rani Laksmibai, the last ruler of Jhansi who bravely fought and died at the hands of the British in 1858 when they tried to annex her kingdom and bring it under the British rule. In Jhansi, we visited my favourite aunt whose son and daughter had met and welcomed Margaret when she landed in Bombay only a few weeks ago. We visited her in her old and sprawling family home whose nooks and crannies I vaguely remembered from previous visits as a small child. My aunt was very gracious and prepared a special dinner to welcome the newly married couple, and she thoroughly approved of my choice for a bride.

A WASP bride in a Hindu household

It was *Diwali* morning when we boarded the train for the next leg of our journey to Hatta, my hometown, and we arrived in Damoh, the nearest train station in the late afternoon. By this time, Margaret was starting to feel quite comfortable wearing a *sari* and preferred it over Western style attire to avoid being too conspicuous in the Indian hinterland. I was not looking forward to the remaining forty kilometre journey by road in a dirty and noisy government-issue bus. Fortunately, as we got off the train in Damoh, I again ran into my 'Good Samaritan' Mr Bajaj, the politician from Hatta who had helped me years ago in Bhopal when I went there to tackle the State Government bureaucracy. He offered us a lift in his jeep which was waiting for him outside the train station and we all piled into the jeep for the 90-minute journey. As we approached my hometown, I began to wonder how this first real and close encounter between the East and the West would play out. Margaret was about to encounter an orthodox Brahmin household consisting of four generations of my family with thousands of years of tradition behind it, in a house located in a remote Indian town with rather primitive facilities compared to even a modest Western residence. Would this encounter lead to mutual understanding, acceptance and goodwill or would it result in disappointment, distrust and disillusionment?

As the jeep came to a stop in front of our house, and Margaret and I entered the front courtyard, most of my family came out to greet us and to get their first glimpse of the new and exotic bride, as did half of the neighbourhood ladies and children who were of course, anxious to get a glimpse of the foreign bride. Both Margaret and I touched my father's feet as well as those of my grandmother and elder sister – the traditional Hindu way of showing respect and soliciting their blessing. It was the evening of the important Hindu festival of *Diwali* and every one in the house was in a festive mood, getting ready for the *Lakshmi Pooja*, worshiping Hindu goddess of wealth and prosperity, the lighting of the earthen lamps around the house and the fireworks that would follow. After we had freshened up, Margaret was escorted to the kitchen and eating area where she sat on a *pata*, the very low wooden stool used for sitting cross legged to eat an Indian meal, surrounded by the ladies of the house, only a couple of whom were able to communicate with her in English. While I do not now recall the exact nature or sequence of events of that evening, I was gratified to observe that my family members seemed quite sympathetic to the predicament of this white young woman from a distant land, who suddenly found herself in a strange old house full of unknown people who had been raised in an entirely different culture and way of life. Of course, there was a level of curiosity and an initial display of formality on their part, but they tried to ensure that Margaret was as comfortable as possible and that all of her immediate physical needs were looked after. With the feast and festivities of a *Diwali* night upon us, the evening went quickly and it was soon bedtime.

We climbed the stairs to the upper level using a small kerosene lamp as a light source – our town had no electricity or running water in 1964. The space where we were to sleep was a large room with windows on all sides. For quite some time we could hear the fireworks exploding in the distant parts of the town. In the morning, we woke up to the sound of the neighbourhood ladies drawing water from the nearby well, and we could see the sun just rising above the eastern horizon. We could hear my father chanting his morning prayers after which he would start milking our cows and buffalos for the daily household supply of milk. By the time we went downstairs and freshened up, my elder sister had lit the *chullah,* to prepare the morning *chai*. Every one seemed to congregate around the *chullah* waiting for the first cup of *chai* of the day before they could get on with any other chores. After morning tea, we spent some time in the rear courtyard where the pomegranate tree was in full bloom with beautiful red flowers and my sister-in-law was busy giving her recently born baby girl her daily massage in the morning sun. The ladies of the house soon started getting ready to prepare the morning meal and my grandmother invited Margaret to join her in preparing the vegetables for the *sabjis* (curried vegetables) which form an integral part of an Indian vegetarian meal. Later in the morning Margaret and I accompanied my elder sister and some other family members to visit our family temple which was only a few yards away to join in the daily worship of our family deity and to seek her blessing as a newlywed couple – a long standing tradition in the family. The following day we had to leave for Jabalpur since the Engineering College was about to start its winter term and all teaching staff were required to be present on the first, and last, day of term.

Married life in an Indian town

We both regretted that our stay with the family was so short and hoped to stay longer on our next visit. In one way however, it was fortunate that we left when we did, because on the evening we left, Margaret started her menstrual period. The traditional practice in our family was to isolate or quarantine menstruating ladies, which would have led to an awkward situation. For the trip to Jabalpur we had to travel in a noisy and crowded old bus which took almost five hours to cover a distance of 150 km. It stopped frequently to pick up passengers waiting on the roadside, and ultimately broke down half way to the destination, forcing us to wait for the next bus on the route to come along. In the late evening, we finally arrived at the little bungalow in the Engineering College campus that would be our first home as husband and wife. As they say 'the honeymoon was over' and I was ready to start the next phase of my life with a lot of hope and some lingering unease about how this union of East and West would unfold. After a quick dinner which we had brought with us from home, we went to visit the Deshpandes to let them know that we were back and were looking forward to enjoying our life in the college campus. Mrs. Deshpande kindly offered to come over next day to help Margaret settle down into her new home and to provide some welcome advice on how to live happily in a servant- intensive household.

Soon the winter term at the college started and our life began to settle into a routine that essentially revolved around the hours that I was required to spend at the college conducting lectures and labs between 10:00 am and 5:00 pm, six days a week. First thing in the morning the milkman knocked at the door to deliver the daily supply of buffalo milk. He was followed by the arrival of Pandit, our cook whose first job of the day was to boil the milk and prepare the morning tea. Next to show up was the newspaper man on his bike, delivering the local Hindi paper and the Times of India which carried national and international news. He also carried a selection of popular Hindi magazines which interested housewives could borrow for a couple of days for a small rental fee. After our morning ritual of reading the newspapers while having tea, I usually spent the next hour or so reviewing my lecture and lab assignments for the day. Margaret would bathe and change into a fresh *sari* and usually spend some time in the kitchen observing Pandit while he cooked dishes for our breakfast and lunch, in order to learn the basics of Indian vegetarian cooking. After having my bath followed by breakfast with Margaret, I left for the college a little after 9:30 am (obviously no kissing good bye at the front gate), to return home for a short break around noon for the lunch that Pandit had prepared.

The staff colony was a microcosm of a small isolated Indian village, with a bit more modern infrastructure and housing. The population in the college staff colony was generally divided not by caste but by class. Class was determined by whether you were a member of the teaching or senior administrative staff, the technical support staff, administrative support staff or the servant class that catered to the needs of the households of the teaching class. Although almost every one lived within a half-mile radius, there was very little social mingling across class boundaries, and any contact was on a need only basis. However, as to be expected, within the classes, there was also an additional affinity among members of the same ethnic/geographic groups (e.g., Bengalis, Gujaratis, Maharashtrians, South Indians, and Punjabis etc.). This was particularly evident among the teaching and senior administrative staff which was very diverse and represented almost all major regions of the country. Our own position in this hierarchy was obvious and most of our social interactions and friendships were confined to the members of the teaching and senior administrative staff who lived in the staff colony or in the city of Jabalpur. Many of them had pursued higher studies in the West. A few of them, like Professor Deshpande, had met Margaret while she was in Canada, and they made a special effort to seek our company often to reminisce about their experiences in the West and exchange views on social, cultural and political issues within a wider global context. Needless to say, Margaret was viewed as the local expert on all things Western and was frequently consulted on topics that ranged from explaining the meaning behind Alexander Pope's early eighteenth century poem 'The Rape of the Lock' to a friend's son, a student at a local college, to advising prospective visitors to the West on how best to navigate Western society during their stay abroad. She also had to console a young man who had fallen in love with a girl from a Western country and was in a similar dilemma as I had faced. But in his case he was already married (not just engaged) to a girl in India – there being a large leap between breaking an engagement and breaking the marriage vows, he reluctantly reconciled himself to maintaining the status quo.

In the absence of modern conveniences such as a telephone, radio, television or motorized vehicle, our daily life in the isolated enclave moved at a slow and serene pace. Most evenings, we would go for a walk around the staff colony or to the lake behind the College and more often than not end up dropping in, unannounced, or being invited to some friend's house for the inevitable cups of tea and talk. With no means of personal transport, our trips to the city centre to visit friends and colleagues, or to see an English movie at the Empire theatre were few and far between. One of the movies we watched was Dr Zhivago, which was filled with scenes of vast snow-covered landscapes, mostly filmed in the Canadian prairies. Coming out of the theatre after the movie into a completely different Indian landscape with the air temperature hovering around 40 degrees Celsius, was particularly disorienting for Margaret. The film sparked a sense of nostalgia for her rural Ontario homestead which in winter would be surrounded by pristine snow as far as one could see, as well as nostalgia for many sleigh rides she had enjoyed as a child.

One afternoon in late November we noticed a bullock cart coming around the road carrying a large 8'x4'x4' crate. When it stopped in front of our house, we realised that it was the shipment sent by Margaret's family in Canada which had finally made its way across the world travelling by various forms of transport – the last leg of which was on a bullock cart from the local railway station to our house. With the help of a gang of servants, the crate was unloaded and brought inside for unpacking. In addition to many household and personal items, the crate yielded a 16 cubic foot copper coloured refrigerator – probably the only one of its kind and size not only in the city of Jabalpur but in the whole province – which was a wedding gift from Margaret's two brothers. The items also included a twelve place-setting of Wedgewood china and a silver cutlery set to go with the Wedgwood china, a Limoges tea service that had originally belonged to Margaret's grandmother, a large number of very delicate china teacups and saucers, including half a dozen Irish Belleek pieces, and a five-tier wedding cake made by her sister-in-law encased in solid white icing and laced generously with brandy (as a preservative). In order to protect the extremely fragile items for the long journey, the packers in Canada had wrapped each item in extra layers of paper and by the time everything was unpacked and put away, our large courtyard was full of paper. The servants had a field day fighting over the discarded paper which they would sell to the paper recycling man who came around every week on his bicycle to buy old newspapers which he made into paper bags and in turn sold to local shop keepers for packing every day household products.

The refrigerator was a great success with the neighbourhood kids, as well as with my nephews and nieces who visited in the summer months. They liked to raid the refrigerator not for food (it was mostly filled with bottles of cold water and a few other items) but for the ice cubes which they would put in their mouths to relish the cold, clean taste. However, the fine china and silver cutlery was rarely brought out for use because Indian food is best eaten and enjoyed using one's right hand – according to an often quoted statement, sometimes attributed to Jawahar Lal Nehru our first Prime Minister, "eating Indian food with cutlery is like making love through an interpreter". Another reason for our reluctance to use the china was the underlying fear that the servants who mostly did the daily washing of dishes and utensils could not be trusted to handle the expensive china properly and safely. However, all the imported china and cutlery were put to good use when we threw a 'wedding cake cutting' party for our friends, colleagues and neighbours a few days after the arrival of the big crate from Canada. Everyone relished the taste of the wedding cake in spite of its high alcohol content and it seems none of them suffered any ill effects.

Besides the Deshpande family, we also became very close to the family of Mr. S.R. Pandya, the Administrative Registrar of the College. Mr. S.R. Pandya belonged to my Gujarati community. He came from a small village not far from my hometown and was also a distant relative. His family had taken me under their wing soon after I joined the teaching faculty at the College and were now living in a neighbouring bungalow. Having worked as a Government bureaucrat all his life, he was thoroughly conversant with all the Government's administrative rules and regulations – most of them enacted during the British Raj. Like a Bible scholar who can produce scriptural backing for or against any moral or ethical issue at hand, he could quote appropriate sections from Government manuals to justify any intended action on a file. However, on a personal level, he and his wife and six children were very pleasant and generous in providing support to me and especially to Margaret who was learning to navigate in an unfamiliar culture and a socio-economic environment which was markedly different from Canada. One of the first and perhaps wisest decisions that Margaret made was to hire Mrs. Fernandez, a Goan lady married to a member of the Technical Support staff at the college, to give her lessons in the basics of written and spoken Hindi, which helped her to acquire a degree of conversational capability in the local language. Soon Margaret started to get together with Mrs. S.R. Pandya and Mrs. Dubova, the wife of one of the two visiting professors from Russia at the College, for late morning tea. Since none of them spoke or understood each other's language, I have always wondered how they communicated with each other.

Our first Christmas in India as a married couple was a rather low key affair. The city of Jabalpur has a significant population of Christians, and a number of schools, colleges, churches and other institutions are run through their charitable trusts, including the large campus of St Leonard Theological College which trains indigenous graduates for Christian ministries. In India, a secular state with a significant population of Christians Christmas is a national holiday and it is enthusiastically celebrated in larger cities and towns all across the country. However, our staff colony was far from the city and rather isolated, with only a few Christian families – mostly transplants from places like Goa and Kerala in south western India, with whom we had very little social contact. Although both Margaret and I had been brought up in the prevailing religious environments of our cultures (Protestant Christian and Hindu, respectively), neither of us were very dogmatic about our religious beliefs or practices. For both of us, religious holidays were mostly social occasions for renewing our ties with family and friends against the backdrop of some traditional religious rituals and symbols. That year, our Christmas consisted primarily of decorating a little tree in a pot and inviting our friends for an evening of food and drink. We opened Christmas presents sent by Margaret's relatives and friends in Canada, and exchanged our modest gifts picked from the limited choice available in the city. Both of us were feeling nostalgic for the last Christmas we spent together at her family farm in Ontario. There, we had enjoyed all the trappings and rituals of a traditional white Christmas, made picture perfect by the sight of Margaret's young nephews and nieces, anxiously waiting for Santa Claus to arrive with his surprise gifts.

CHAPTER 10

Eastern realities challenge Western learning

Planning for the pregnancy

Soon after the start of the New Year we learned that Margaret was expecting a child. This news was a much more exciting and wonderful gift than any we had ever received. However, at this early stage, we had not thought through the practicalities of managing the progression from pregnancy, to childbirth and beyond. My own cultural background and experience was of little help because in our community and many others in India, for the first couple of pregnancies, the young bride goes to her parents' family who look after all her needs until she and the newborn baby are ready to move back to the marital home. The practice was grounded in a number of factors which included: the tradition of arranged marriages for girls at puberty, pregnancies at an early age and extended family living. The assumption was that the newlywed woman has not yet been fully assimilated within her husband's extended family and is likely to feel more comfortable and less stressed during the birthing process, in a more familiar atmosphere, where her loving parents, siblings and close relatives at her side. No wonder many of our Indian friends felt sorry for Margaret because she was unable to go home to her mother to have her first baby.

In Western countries now, most, though not all, babies are born in a hospital which is well equipped to handle any medical complications which may arise during the birthing process. The whole process from early pregnancy to birth and beyond takes place under the guidance of a qualified physician. The parents-to-be are of course, the primary drivers of the process and generally care for the infant at home, with some assistance provided by their respective families during the first couple of months. India, on the other hand, continues to be a country of mostly small, scattered villages with minimal medical facilities. In India, except for large towns and cities, the majority of births still take place at home with the assistance of close female family members and the village birthing lady whose basic skills are passed on from one generation to another. Fortunately, Jabalpur was a large enough city and a major population centre and had a number of medical facilities including a degree-awarding College of Medicine. These medical institutions were adequate, but nowhere near the standards of service and care available in a city of comparable size in a Western country. For maternity care, one of our options was the public hospital for women, which was established during the British Raj and was still called Lady Elgin Hospital. It provided care in the areas of obstetrics and gynaecology as well as paediatrics and was also affiliated with the local College of Medicine. The other choices included a couple of private (for profit) maternity clinics with limited staff (one physician and a few nurses) and facilities geared primarily towards delivering babies and had limited capabilities to handle any major complications. The private clinics' clientele was largely confined to well-to-do families who could afford to pay for somewhat more personalized services. We decided in favour of the Lady Elgin Hospital because of its wider range of staff (in quantity and quality) and services, and its affiliation with the Medical School as a teaching hospital. As well, the wife of one of my colleagues at the Engineering College who lived in the staff colony was a staff physician at the hospital and she readily agreed to be Margaret's attending obstetrician.

Through the winter months the pregnancy progressed normally with the usual bouts of morning sickness and intense cravings for items like a hamburger or a peanut butter sandwich. Getting a Western style hamburger was a non-starter – McDonalds was still a long way from invading India and even when they arrived, beef hamburgers were not on their menu – the majority of India's population is vegetarian and among those who are not, Hindus avoid beef and Muslims avoid pork on religious grounds. Peanut butter was not a commodity widely available in India at the time and certainly not in a town like Jabalpur. My frantic search in local shops produced a jar of the stuff which had probably been sitting on the shelf forever.

Around early March we encountered our first worrisome episode when Margaret started some noticeable bleeding and we were afraid it might lead to a miscarriage. We immediately consulted her obstetrician who ordered complete bed rest for a few days, advising her to elevate legs and torso during the time. Fortunately the bleeding soon stopped and we were both greatly relieved that the baby had not been lost at mid term. After the follow up examination by her obstetrician we were assured that the baby was developing normally and that the crisis was, hopefully, behind us.

Margaret's first summer in India

March was the beginning of the short spring season in our region, a time when the breezes start getting warmer, the flowering trees are loaded, spreading their sweet fragrance, and the *Gulmohar* and *Palash* trees are in full bloom displaying bright yellow and red colours. As a child growing up in my small town, I used to look forward to the arrival of this season because at this time the *Mahua* trees would bloom each night and their sweet and juicy barrel-shaped white flowers would drop on the ground very early in the morning. My friends and I would wake up early and roam the local woods and farms in search of these trees so that we could eat our fill of the sweet flowers before sunrise. As the day progressed along with the warmth of the sun the *Mahua* flowers would start to ferment and could cause a bad headache, if eaten after sun got hot. Many ladies from poorer homes in our neighbourhood would go out and collect these flowers which were then put out to dry in the sun and later used as a sweetener in cooking. They were also collected in large quantities by licensed outfits that manufactured local liquor. The *Mahua* flowers would be dried, fermented and distilled into rather foul-tasting local hooch sold in country liquor shops.

By the end of April the summer's dry heat had truly started, with daytime temperatures hovering in the 40 degree Celsius range. We had, of course, no air conditioning and the only relief from the heat was from a small electric fan. During the summer nights, as in most North Indian households, we slept out under the stars in our enclosed private courtyard which we would sprinkle liberally with water every evening to cool it down. Students were busy writing their end of year examinations and the teaching faculty was looking forward to the annual summer vacation that spanned the months of May and June.

During the hot summer months the landscape changed and everything became brown and dusty with frequent dust storms. Our day-to-day routine also changed in order to cope with the hot weather. We finished all our morning activities including our meal by 11.00, closed all of the doors and windows, drew the shades and curtains and retired to our bedroom to spend most of the day reading and/or sleeping under the fan. We would also hang mats made of a special grass called *Khus Khus* on the bedroom doors, which when sprayed with water not only cooled down the inside air but also added a pleasant fragrance. We only emerged from our hibernation when our cook arrived at around 5:00 pm to prepare the afternoon tea. After the tea and a cooling bath we would venture out for a walk returning home to sit in our courtyard or the front garden watching the chameleons and geckos trying to catch insects, until the cook announced that the dinner was ready to be served.

In May, a group of my young nieces and nephews arrived to spend some time with us and to get better acquainted with their Canadian auntie. They were all good natured, inquisitive children who were fascinated by many of Margaret's Western belongings which they had never seen before, including such items as the fine china and sterling silver, her high heeled shoes and elbow-length white gloves. However, the large refrigerator was their favourite and frequent target not only for the bottles of ice cold water but also for the ice cubes that they could munch on. At night they all slept on a row of beds in the front garden where under the moonlit sky, one of our favourite nieces would entertain every one with bedtime stories from the *Panchtantra*, the third century BCE collection of Indian animal fables, which she had probably learned from her mother and grandmother. Some of these tales are said to have been told by Buddha himself as a way of imparting moral values to his disciples. We also hosted a series of other house guests including my cousin from Bombay at whose bungalow Margaret had stayed upon her arrival in India.

A premature birth

Having grown up on a farm in Ontario, Margaret had been brought up with the high standards of hospitality common to a rural community of pioneer settlers. She welcomed the opportunity to entertain our visitors through the summer as well as the opportunity to have closer contact with my relatives and friends. However, in spite of the extra help provided by our servants, the combination of the unfamiliar summer heat and the increasing discomfort of advancing pregnancy started to take its toll. As the month of June approached, a prolonged period of exceptionally intense heat began, with maximum temperatures hovering well over 40 degrees Celsius. Unaccustomed to such hot and dry weather and unable to cope with it in her current stage of pregnancy, Margaret suffered severe fluid loss, diminished appetite and a drop in blood pressure. The obstetrician examined her and placed her on medication and ordered modified bed rest. In spite of this care, Margaret started to have contractions on the afternoon of June 14, 1965. Unfortunately, her regular obstetrician was on sick leave and she advised us to immediately consult the Chief Obstetrician at the Lady Elgin Hospital. Professor Deshpande kindly drove us down to the physician's consulting clinic that evening where he injected some medication to stave off the potential premature birth. He also admitted her into the hospital and left necessary instructions with the hospital staff for her further care.

Considering that the contractions had eased and that Margaret was in the best possible place in case she needed further medical care, I bunked in for the night at the house of a colleague and friend who lived not far from the hospital. The next morning I borrowed his scooter, picked up some breakfast for Margaret – the hospital did not serve meals and the patient's relatives were responsible for them – and arrived at the hospital thinking that she might be released from the hospital and the two of us could go home. To my great surprise, Margaret told me that early that morning, I had become the father of a ten-week prematurely born baby boy weighing three pounds and two ounces. I was not really prepared for this news and my immediate reaction and feelings were a mixed bag. On one hand, I was happy that we had a son albeit greatly premature and fragile. On the other, I did not have a clue how we were going to care for such a small and fragile baby by ourselves, knowing that very special protocols and procedures would be required to ensure his survival. I knew that the hospital was not well equipped for the long-term care of premature babies, and that after a few days in the nursery for premature babies, our son would be released in our care. Unlike Western hospitals, the nursery for premature babies where our son was transferred did not have any incubators or any climate control facilities. However, it did impose strict protocols to maintain good hygiene and isolation regime to avoid undue exposure to the babies. It was supervised by the resident paediatrician and we were glad that he agreed to look after our son not only while he was in the hospital nursery but also for follow-up care after his discharge.

Margaret was provided with a large private room which had an extra cot for one of the patient's relatives (me, in this case) who would look after her non-medical needs, including providing meals. Her room faced the nursery for premature infants across the central courtyard and she had to walk down every two hours to breastfeed our son, who fortunately was developing good rooting and sucking instincts after a few days of feeding by a dropper. Since the hospital was a long way from our home on the Engineering College campus and there were no good, dependable restaurants nearby, I wondered how I would manage to provide a regular supply of three meals a day. Fortunately, the paediatrician came to our rescue and introduced us to his friend, Dr. Carlos Welsh, an American Methodist minister who was on the staff of the Leonard Theological College and lived on its campus not far from the hospital. Dr. Welsh and his wife who happened to be the sister of the Manager of the YMCA in Nainital where we had spent our honeymoon, kindly offered to send us home-cooked meals while Margaret was in the hospital. We really appreciated their generosity and Christian spirit, and became good friends with the Welsh family, visiting them often until they finally returned to America.

Home care of a premature baby

During our stay at the hospital, the monsoon broke with its usual sound and fury and brought strong winds and heavy rain which flooded the hospital's central courtyard. The monsoon rain finally brought some welcome relief from the oppressive heat of the last days of summer. After a stay of about ten days, as expected, Margaret and our son were discharged from the hospital. A few days before the discharge, we started to plan for home care for him. Although Margaret was a fully qualified nurse from a highly-rated hospital in Toronto and had a Diploma in Public Health Nursing from the University of Toronto, her text books and previous work experience with premature babies were of little help. Her training and experience were in hospitals where such babies were isolated in a climate- controlled incubator in well-equipped nurseries. We decided on a plan that would essentially replicate the conditions of the nursery at the Lady Elgin Hospital in terms of cleanliness, hygiene, and isolation. To this end, we thoroughly cleaned our spare bedroom and emptied it except for a baby crib, a cot for Margaret, a chair for breastfeeding, and the items essential for maintaining a proper level of hygiene and cleanliness. The room was off limits to anyone but the parents and the paediatrician who came for regular weekly home visits to check on the baby's progress. Margaret's nursing background and training in Public Health were critical in creating the best possible home care situation for our premature son, in a place where sophisticated equipment of any kind was hard, if not impossible, to come by.

We put off choosing a name for our son until he had reached his normal birth weight and had overcome any other developmental deficiencies caused by his premature arrival. In the interim, we decided to call him 'Nath' which is a middle name commonly used in my family. Fortunately, except for a couple of panic-inducing emergencies, he recovered from any effects of his premature birth within two months. The first emergency occurred on our sixth day home which also happened to be the first day of the academic term at the College and my first day at work after the summer vacation. Margaret was alone at home with our son for the first time after returning from the hospital and I decided to come home for lunch a bit early to spend some extra time with them. As soon as I walked in the door, I saw that there was a serious problem with the baby and Margaret was obviously deeply concerned and in a state of near panic. It seemed that the baby had regurgitated, with some yellow frothy fluid issuing from his nose and the baby was rapidly becoming cyanosed. It was obvious that immediate clearing of his nasal passage was critical for his survival and Margaret was frantically searching for a way to achieve this. Fortunately, I remembered that I had recently bought an ink dropper which worked on a suction principle, like a miniature turkey baster used in Western kitchens. I quickly handed it to Margaret who used it to successfully suck all of the fluid from the baby's nasal passage and his colour gradually returned from almost black to red to normal. We called the paediatrician who came over in the afternoon and after thoroughly examining the baby announced that his lungs were clear of any fluid and there was no evidence of any damage. In his opinion, the baby had probably regurgitated his feeding with some force that sent some of it through his nose, and since premature babies are unable to breath through their mouths, he started becoming cyanotic when his air passage was blocked.

To some extent, the source of the second emergency was related to the first one in that Margaret was in constant fear that the baby would regurgitate again, and she failed to get enough sleep and became exhausted. One morning she woke with such severe nausea and vomiting that we got concerned and on a local doctor's advice, she took a dose of anti-nausea medication without realizing that some of it might be passed on to the baby through breastfeeding. Suddenly in the evening she noticed that the baby was turning a deadly whitish-blue colour. Since we were unable to phone the paediatrician, a neighbourhood friend who had a car drove us to the hospital where they pumped the baby's stomach and administered oxygen. Although he spent an uneventful night at the hospital, he became cyanotic again the next morning and required prompt treatment from the hospital staff. At the paediatrician's suggestion, the three of us moved into a private room in the hospital. As per prevailing practice in the hospital, the nurses visited the baby frequently to provide professional care, but the rest of our needs – meals, medications and administering oral medications for the baby – were our responsibility. We stayed in the hospital for four days during which there was no recurrence of cyanosis and the paediatrician felt that our son had fully recovered and was ready for discharge. According to the paediatrician, the episode was probably triggered by a small quantity of the anti-nausea drug getting into his system which in turn caused some sedation and which further weakened his immature swallowing reflex, leading to aspiration.

All is well that ends well

Needless to say, Margaret's background in nursing and her ability to appropriately adapt her Western learning to the Eastern realities played a pivotal role in our son's care and survival. A few other factors worked in our favour, as well. For example, the arrival of the monsoon rains soon after his birth were a godsend in that they brought welcome relief from the intense, dry summer heat, heralding a season of cooler temperatures and higher humidity. Although it was still not ideal, this change to a cooler, more humid climate created an atmosphere more conducive to a premature baby's comfort and contributed to our son's recovery. We were also very grateful for the unconditional moral and material support we received from our friends and neighbours in the staff colony at critical periods during his care. Lastly, we were lucky in the choice of a paediatrician for our son who not only displayed a high level of professional competence, but also offered counselling and moral support to us at times of uncertainty and acute anxiety.

After the last emergency visit to the hospital, the next couple of months went quietly without any significant setbacks. By mid-August, the baby had gained sufficient weight and all of his physical and mental faculties seemed to have matured to normal levels with no apparent deficiencies. We celebrated his "birth" day on August 15th, first by moving the mother and child into our main bedroom and second by finally choosing a permanent name. We decided to call him Ravindra (Ravi) Nath after Rabindranath Tagore, the Bengali poet and writer, who won the Nobel Prize in literature for Gitanjali, a collection of his poems. Ravi started off by sleeping in a simple crib that also served as a swing, with a cord that we could pull from our bed. If he became restless during the night, I would activate the swing and more often than not the gentle swinging motion would put him back to sleep. When he outgrew the crib, in accordance with prevailing Indian tradition, he started sharing our bed and continued to do so until he was three years old. By the time October and the *Diwali* holiday season arrived, his continued progress towards normal growth gave us the confidence to undertake the arduous bus journey to my ancestral home for the *Diwali*. festival. There, we proudly showed off our first born to my family and visiting our family temple to offer prayers to our family deity for a happy ending to the worrisome period between Ravi's premature birth and his full recovery.

CHAPTER 11

Family life in India: adjustment and consolidation

Life in the slow lane

The next three years were a period of relative calm and tranquility in our life as a family. We gradually slid into the slow pace of daily life partly resulting from the climate and further aided by the scarcity or complete absence of modern conveniences such as telephones, automobiles and television. A trip into the city centre to visit friends or see a movie via a hired bicycle rickshaw meant almost an hour of travel each way. To consult with a colleague or friend living a short distance away in the staff colony, the only option was to show up at his or her door unannounced which more often than not, ended up in a session of drinking tea and exchanging latest gossip. Though at times the scarcity of essential items, such as baby formula or cooking gas, was frustrating, the strong cooperative spirit and sense of community in our little academic enclave, and the ever present support from family and friends made our day-to-day life very pleasant and highly fulfilling.

As parents of a growing child, our lives were especially enriched by the fact that we were living in a very child-friendly environment, which is not unusual in older cultures like India. It was truly heartening to see that from a very young age Ravi's upbringing was not confined to our nuclear family but included the larger group of our extended family, friends and neighbours. Both Margaret and I had grown up in socially well connected rural communities. As Ravi started to treat many of the homes in our neighbourhood as his second home where he was assured of unconditional love and care, we appreciated that the often repeated maxim *"it takes a village to raise a child"* was being played out in our son's upbringing. Quite often the teenage girls in the neighbourhood would take him out for walks and take him home where he would stay for hours entertaining the family – in the paucity of other modern means of entertainment like radio and television, children were often viewed as a great source of entertainment by the families.

Our life revolved mostly around bringing up our son and entertaining and being entertained by a wide group of family, friends and colleagues. In addition to reading and corresponding regularly with her family and friends in Canada, Margaret wrote articles that were published in *The Times of India*, a national English language newspaper. She also wrote an article for The Journal of the Canadian Nurses Organization describing, from the perspective of nursing practices, the home care of Ravi, our prematurely born son. I often teased her about the latter article insinuating that she published the article to allay any hometown gossip about giving birth to our son so soon after her arrival and marriage in India.

During these years, our travel was restricted to annual visits to my ancestral home for *Diwali* holidays or to neighbouring cites to visit close relatives. As well, a number of family and friends stayed with us as guests for varying periods of time. One of our guests was Marjorie, the mutual friend who had introduced Margaret and me in Toronto, launching us on our unorthodox journey. Marjorie was on her way back from a year in Japan where she had been teaching English and, more importantly, reconnecting with her Japanese heritage. Professor Sanyal, one of my former teachers from Calcutta University who was visiting Jabalpur for an academic assignment, was another memorable house guest. He had been educated in England and had lived there for a number of years and seemed to have acquired the mannerism of a *pukka sahib*. For example, we were very intrigued and impressed by his dexterity in eating Indian meals with a knife and fork.

Our contact with the West was mostly limited to letters from Margaret's family and friends from Canada and relevant articles in papers about Europe and North America, although rarely any relating to Canada. The only expatriate American we knew and whose family we frequently visited in Jabalpur was Carlos Welsh, the faculty member at the local Theological College. Jabalpur was not one of the major national tourist sites nor was it an important cultural or historic centre, so the probability of running into visitors from the West was very low, although not non-existent. For example, while attending a friend's wedding reception, we came across a couple of young travellers from Canada. Indian weddings and wedding receptions are generally large, elaborate, noisy and very informal affairs, where there is no such thing as a precise and closed guest list. It is not uncommon for a formally invited guest to bring along his family, including children, as well as one or two friends. The Canadian visitors were most likely the guests of one of their newly acquired friends in Jabalpur who thought these Canadian visitors might enjoy the experience of observing an Indian wedding. Since we did not have the opportunity to socialise with the Canadian visitors during the wedding festivities, we invited them to our house for dinner next evening. During dinner Margaret became convinced that she had seen one of the Canadian visitors some time in the recent past. After a little back and forth about their recent mutual history, it turned out that the young man had been living in a house diagonally across from Margaret's last residence in the Annex neighbourhood in Toronto, and that their paths must have crossed routinely during that time. We were astonished to learn this fact and have always wondered about the odds of such a rare coincidental meeting.

I found it fascinating and greatly satisfying to see how easily Margaret was adapting and starting to feel comfortable in an environment where modern amenities and goods were so rare and where the cultural and religious practices were so different from her own. The fact that she could converse in English with most people was a great help, although she had also gradually picked up some basic Hindi vocabulary. Margaret did not seem particularly bothered by the scarcity of goods and services which were readily available in the West – probably because as a child, she had lived through strict rationing during the war, and had also heard her parents' tales of acute and prolonged deprivation during the Great Depression. The assimilation process was also greatly facilitated by her generous and caring nature and by the unconditional acceptance and true affection that she received from my family and friends.

Thoughts of a Canadian visit

As the year 1968 approached, our thoughts started to wander towards life beyond our current peaceful existence in a largely closed environment. We were approaching a critical turning point where we had to make a choice between continuing with our current comfortable routine, in which the days and seasons repeated themselves with predictable regularity, and looking beyond the confines of this lifestyle to explore opportunities that would widen our professional, social and cultural boundaries. Over the last few years, our life in the slow lane had not only been desirable, but had also been necessary to allow us to recover from the trauma of Ravi's premature birth and his early care under less then ideal conditions. However, Ravi had now developed into a robust, intelligent and alert toddler with no residual symptoms of his premature birth. He had reached a stage of development which placed no restrictions on our emerging plans to spend at least a few years in North America where I could pursue a Doctorate and Margaret could re-enter the nursing profession. We also felt that this would give Ravi an opportunity to meet his extended family in Canada and learn about the relatives whom he had only known in the abstract as the senders of gift parcels that he had received regularly over the past few years.

Having made up our minds to divert from our current course, we started exploring suitable options: admission to a Doctoral program for me and a nursing position for Margaret, in a place within reasonable distance from her family home in Ontario. We had almost decided on the University of Michigan in the United States, where I had been offered admission in the Graduate School and Margaret had been offered a position in the University Hospital. However, we soon began to have misgivings as the news of serious unrest in the States spread around the world following the assassination of Martin Luther King Jr. and Robert F. Kennedy in April and June of 1968 respectively, the former triggering extended rioting in dozens of U.S. cities. Further, poisonous views of politicians like George Wallace and many of his followers gave us cause for concern. We decided to change our plans in favour of Carleton University in Ottawa, a city where Margaret was quickly able to secure a position as a visiting Public Health Nurse.

Having made this decision, the next and perhaps much more difficult task was dealing with the sheer logistics of the move which involved tackling the stifling layers of bureaucracy for essential requirements, such as a leave of absence, passports, visas, and permission to travel abroad, not to mention scrounging enough cash for the airfare. We had to visit the Canadian High Commission in Delhi to arrange for visas for Ravi and me, and there we saw the new Canadian national flag, with the red maple leaf, for the first time – very distinctive and very Canadian. Since I was married to a Canadian citizen, the person in charge of issuing visas at the High Commission suggested that it would be easier and faster to obtain a 'Permanent Resident Visa' for me and our son, rather than a temporary 'Student Visa'. And so it happened that the permanent resident status on which we travelled back to Canada was more a result of expediency than a conscious decision on my part.

To raise enough cash for our airfare, we had no other option but to sell most of the fine Wedgewood and Belleek china and other household items that Margaret had brought from Canada as part of her trousseau. It took a lot of time, energy, perseverance and patience to accomplish these tasks, including frequent trips to the State and the National capital to chase the bureaucracy. However, no task was as difficult as convincing my family – especially my father, that our plans for the next few years were necessary for my professional development and personal happiness. Obviously, their main concern was that this short-term move to Canada might turn into a permanent one. Their concerns were some what alleviated after we convinced them that we had no intention of staying in Canada after my Doctoral studies were completed.

And so, the stage was set for our trip to Canada and by early August we were anxiously waiting for the day of our departure in the first week of September. However, the whole plan almost came to a screeching halt, when Margaret informed me that she had missed her menstrual period and there was a good likelihood that she was pregnant. We immediately consulted her physician who prescribed some medication to induce the menstrual flow. She also suggested that in case the medications were ineffective, she would be willing to arrange for a quick D&C procedure – if that is what we wanted. Fortunately, we were spared from making such a difficult decision because the medication had the desired effect within a few days. We breathed a great sigh of relief and put our plans back on track. After this unexpected bump in our path, the remaining time to our departure date passed quickly and uneventfully, and, after a brief visit to my ancestral home to say goodbye to my family, we left for Delhi to catch our flight.

It was a conscious decision on our part to change course at this juncture in our life, leaving behind the reasonably stable and pleasant lifestyle that we were enjoying in India. We had been living in a close knit community of family and friends which, in retrospect we realise was a blessing on several levels. First of all, it provided a very secure, loving and nurturing environment in which our son could grow into a well-adjusted toddler. Secondly, as a full and respected member of my family and the community of friends and colleagues, Margaret had the time and opportunity to experience the subtle nuances of an ancient and complex culture from a close range – a privilege rarely available to a person from the West. Margaret, to her credit, took full advantage of the opportunity to establish long lasting connections with my extended family and forge friendships that have endured over time and distance. Most importantly, during the early years of our marriage, we went through periods of extreme anxiety, as well as periods of great happiness and contentment, which tested our commitment to each other. That commitment ultimately helped us to establish a family dynamic which, has served us well and has guided us over the periods of ups and downs which we inevitably encountered in the future.

This intentional diversion in the direction of our journey represented a major change from our current environment and life style. We were moving from the East to the West, from a country of intense heat and dust storms to one noted for extreme cold and snowstorms, from a developing country dogged by scarcities, to a fully developed country blessed with an over abundance of everything. Further, my professional role was shifting from a teacher used to facing a class of students to a student facing the white board. Margaret was changing her role from a housewife with many servants to a working woman with only limited help available from inanimate gadgets. Ravi was moving from individualized, personal care at home in a familiar community that he trusted, to some kind of external and, hopefully, professional, group care environment. Our excitement and anticipation about the venture was therefore tempered with a degree of uncertainty and apprehension. Were we too optimistic to hope that the next few years would play out as we expected? And if not, were we prepared for unforeseen challenges and setbacks that might come our way? We did not have to wait very long before we got an inkling of the rough waters ahead.

CANADA (1968 – 1972)

****

CHAPTER 12

A rough start to the new adventure

Our travel agent had arranged an itinerary that included a complimentary stay at a London hotel near Buckingham Palace for a couple of nights. We were met at Heathrow airport by one of Margaret's friends living in London, and spent most of next day visiting a few sights in London and taking Ravi for a ride on a London Double Decker bus. This was his first exposure to a large Western metropolis and Western culture. The whole scene must have been rather strange and somewhat confusing for him – especially when he saw men on the street wearing kilts and women in pant suits. Things looked rather unfamiliar to us as well, what with young women in mini skirts and young men displaying long bushy sideburns. We spent the second evening in London with another friend from the University of Toronto, who travelled from Cardiff to meet us. The next afternoon we boarded our flight to Toronto where Margaret's family was waiting for us at the airport. After spending the night at her cousin's house nearby, we left for Lindsay to spend a few days with Margaret's family before leaving for Ottawa, our final destination.

Settling in to a new life style

Margaret's brother drove us to Peterborough where we caught a Grey Line bus to Ottawa. The journey took over four hours, travelling along Highway 7, with stops at small eastern Ontario farm towns along the way. We arrived at the Albert Street Bus Depot in Ottawa in the late evening and booked into a small hotel on Nicholas Street for the night. The hotel was almost next door to the old County Jail, which is now used as a Youth Hostel. The next morning, I phoned our old friends Bob and Elaine, hoping that they could help us settle into a city with which we had only a passing acquaintance. Bob and Elaine very graciously invited us to stay with them until we could make more permanent living arrangements. Since we had seen them last, also in Ottawa almost four years ago, they now had two children and had moved into an old clapboard house just outside Stittsville, a small village located beyond the western fringe of Ottawa. Although the house was small and located on the main road passing through the village, it was surrounded by open land and woods, providing a pleasant setting for adults and children alike.

We were anxious to get started on setting up a household and finding a suitable arrangement for Ravi's care during the day when both of us would be attending to our respective commitments – I as a full time student and Margaret working with the Victorian Order of Nurses (VON). The next morning, after a brief meeting with my supervisor at the Engineering Faculty, we made our way to the Students' Housing office in search of family accommodation. The University did not own any residences for students with families and the pickings in the neighbourhood were rather slim. Carleton University was a relatively new and growing university, located at some distance from the city centre. There were mostly single family residences with a few multi-family dwellings scattered around. We made a short list of potential candidates and a volunteer from the housing office offered to drive us around to check them out. To our chagrin, at our first choice, which was a nice apartment building close to the campus and public transportation, the manager told us that the management policy did not allow children in the building – although it did allow dogs and cats! We finally settled on an apartment in a new housing complex across from Mooney's Bay off Riverside Drive. Ours was the newest building among four similar ones, surrounded by modest bungalows with a small shopping centre near the entrance to the complex. It was located on a bus route to the city centre and also went past the University campus. Since we did not have time to explore further possibilities, we decided to sign the lease on a two bedroom apartment which overlooked a large parking lot through floor- to-ceiling windows.

Within the next couple of days, Margaret's brothers brought up some of the furniture that she had left behind before leaving for India, plus some additional household items that they could spare. In the meantime, we frantically searched for a suitable daycare facility for Ravi because both of us were to start our new professional commitments in a few days. Again, the choices were limited and we had to settle for a small outfit which was en route to Margaret's workplace. Although it was a hectic week, with the help of Margaret's family and Bob and Elaine, we managed to set up a basic household and were ready to face the challenges of our new life in Ottawa. The first day Margaret started her work at the VON; she dropped Ravi off at the daycare centre and picked him up on her way back. However, within a day or two Ravi became thoroughly disillusioned and unhappy with the atmosphere at the daycare and started showing increasing reluctance to go there. Before the end of the week, one morning, he simply refused to go. This was one of the very rare occasions that I became thoroughly frustrated and ended up spanking him, albeit with no useful results. I stayed home for the next couple of days, while we explored other possibilities for Ravi's care during the work day. We reached the conclusion that the most desirable option was to look for a family in the apartment building, with children of similar ages, who might be interested in earning some extra income by looking after Ravi during the day. We intended to look for a suitable family on the weekend. However, the whole situation changed drastically before we could pursue our plan.

A major setback

On Friday evening we decided to meet in the city after Margaret finished her work day and go to the local Sears store to see if we could buy some curtains for the floor-to-ceiling windows, at least for our bedroom. The store was in the west end of the city and a long bus ride from the city centre. By the time we were ready to return home, it was getting late and we found the bus connections were few and far between. It was almost ten o'clock when a bus finally dropped us on Riverside Drive across from the entrance to our apartment complex. As we were crossing the road in tandem holding hands with Ravi in the middle, a Volkswagen car appeared from our right and hit Margaret full force throwing her almost seventy feet and inflicted a glancing blow to Ravi. Suddenly, it seemed as if our safe and secure little world was about to collapse. Fortunately a police car was in the vicinity and the police officer quickly took charge and we were dispatched in an ambulance to the nearby Riverside hospital. I spent a good part of the night waiting anxiously in the hospital emergency waiting room. Finally, the doctor informed me that though Margaret did not seem to have suffered any major external injuries, he was not sure about any internal injuries, such as a ruptured spleen, and he recommended that she stay in the hospital for further observation and diagnosis. Ravi had only suffered a simple greenstick fracture to his right leg which would have to be in a cast for the next four weeks. Barring any major complications, the doctor felt that Margaret would fully recover in four to six weeks. Our life had suddenly taken an unforeseen turn throwing a significant degree of uncertainty over our plans. I consoled myself with the fact that the outcome could have been much more drastic and thanked my stars for sparing us from what could easily have turned into a greater tragedy. It was also fortunate that we had had the foresight to arrange for a Blue Cross health insurance policy before our arrival in Canada.

The next morning I phoned Margaret's family to tell them about the accident and her current status. By the late afternoon Margaret's mother and her brother arrived in Ottawa. By this time, Ravi had been discharged and barring any adverse developments, Margaret was scheduled to be discharged next day. When she came home, Margaret had no recollection of the accident and was in a state of some confusion about what had happened. To my great relief, her mother and brother insisted that it would be in everyone's best interest if Margaret and Ravi went to stay with them until she had sufficiently recuperated to resume her life in Ottawa. So I was left alone with few friends, trying to fit back into a new life as a graduate student and coping with a normal course load at the University.

The immediate and more critical problem was our finances. Our whole plan for this venture was based on the assumption that Margaret would be the primary breadwinner in the family, supplemented by my research assistantship at the university. So far, neither of us had received any part of our expected earnings and we were managing with money that Margaret's family had kindly advanced to us. I did not feel comfortable in further imposing on their generosity. So, in order to manage this difficult period I had little choice but to borrow funds from the bank – a first in my life. It was a lonely and stressful time and I often wondered whether the decision to leave behind our simple and serene life back in India had been a mistake. However, going back was not an option and the only way was to face the situation as best as we could.

After about four weeks, Margaret felt that she had recovered sufficiently and decided to return to Ottawa with Ravi. Follow up tests indicated that although she had few internal or external residual effects, there was some damage to the optic nerve in one eye which would make driving rather difficult and risky, if not impossible. This deficiency posed a problem because Margaret's position with the VON required that she obtain a driver's license in order to discharge her assigned duties as a visiting nurse which required her to see patients in different parts of the city. Fortunately, the Director of the VON in Ottawa was very sympathetic to our plight. She agreed to assign the so called 'walking district' to Margaret so that she would have patients concentrated around the city centre, where she could walk to visit them. The VON Director also found us a reputable lawyer who was willing to file and represent us on a *pro bono* basis in a civil suit for compensation for pain and suffering from the accident. We also found a nice woman in our apartment building who agreed to look after Ravi along with her own two children during the day. Soon, Margaret started her work with the VON and I started getting into the routine of a graduate student at the University.

A slow recovery

I quickly realized that my experience as a graduate student with a wife and a young child was going to be very different from my last experience. As a graduate student in Toronto more than four years ago, I had been a carefree bachelor and a newcomer to Canada, eager to participate in the activities on and off-campus which had been open for me. According to classic Hindu tradition, a Brahamin's life is divided into four distinct stages or *ashrams,* which follow each other. These consist of *Brahmachari,* the 'student' or 'learning' stage; *Grihastha,* the 'householder' stage; *Sanyasi,* 'retirement and renunciation' stage and ending with *Vanvas,* the 'ascetic' stage of seeking enlightenment and release from the cycle of birth and death. However, combining the so called student and householder stages, as I was now doing, made our life much more hectic and stressful than we had expected. The fact that Margaret had a full-time job which was mentally and physically demanding and that we had barely recovered from the trauma of the recent accident, contributed to our low morale during our first long, cold and miserable Ottawa winter. It took us almost a year to adjust to this new way of life. The support from Margaret's family, and the fact that we made friends with a few more families in the apartment building and established some social life allowed us to recover from the initial rough patch and eased our way into our new, busy life in the West.

During this period, we made friends with a young newly married couple, Barbara and Bruce Baker, who had also moved into our building. Bruce had recently started his teaching career at a local high school with Bob Stevenson, our old friend from Toronto. Bruce was a typical Canadian young man – enthusiastic and ambitious to push ahead in his chosen profession and an avid fan of professional hockey, as well as a keen hockey player. Barbara was a sweet tempered, kind young woman with interests in art and literature. She was fascinated by and immediately bonded with our son Ravi and more or less assumed the role of his unofficial godmother. We spent many weekend evenings in their apartment watching television or playing board games and more often than not, Ravi would fall sleep on their white rug in front of the TV, needing to be carried home to bed at the end of the evening.

Soon, we were in the Christmas season with decorations everywhere and the holiday atmosphere in the air. Although we had celebrated Christmas in India, it was generally a low key affair, consisting of a party with close friends, and exchange of a few simple gifts. This Christmas was the first for Ravi in Canada and he was naturally excited by the snow, the decorations and the festive atmosphere of the season. We were still recovering financially and emotionally from the aftermath of our recent car accident and had to be frugal in our gift giving. After getting a few toys and clothes for Ravi, we had little left over for gifts for each other. The highlight of that Christmas was an evening spent at a 'tree trimming' party at the Stevenson's followed by a family Christmas with Margaret's folks at the farm.

We survived our first Ottawa winter, although it was not a pleasant experience by any means. At the end of a working day, it was hard to cope with the long waits for a bus without any shelter from the bitter cold, biting wind and snow typical of a Canadian winter. By April, we were waiting with open arms to welcome the crocuses whose arrival represented the first sign of spring. With no car of our own, the sphere of our social activities in the winter was confined to visits with the friends we had made in the apartment complex where we lived. With the arrival of warmer weather, and improvement in our cash flow, our social life also improved. Our friends who had cars included us in various excursions in and around the city. We were able to enjoy many barbeques, picnics and open air concerts in the Gatineau Hills across the river and we were all excited while watching the first man landing on the moon, during a trip to visit Margaret's cousin in Montreal. We did not have the time or the resources to take an extended vacation, and so our holidays were confined to a short visit to Margaret's family. Ravi was happy to spend the time with his cousins exploring the open spaces around the farm and swimming in the surrounding Kawartha Lakes. It seemed that the warm weather and the summer days were over too soon and we were heading into the long cold stretch of another Ottawa winter. Besides the friendships we had developed at our apartment complex, we had also made friends through our workplaces, further expanding our social circle and activities. Our financial situation was also on the mend after the initial setback following the car accident. We were looking forward to a relatively easy and smooth sailing for the foreseeable future. Unfortunately, we can never predict the future, nor the timing or nature of the challenges that we may have to face.

CHAPTER 13

Another challenge, recovery and return home

From a socio-economic perspective, our first year in Ottawa was less than satisfactory. Besides coping with the lingering effects of the accident and the unexpected harshness of the Ottawa winter without a car, we were also going through a period of major adjustment. For Margaret, it was a major change from the routine of a stay-at-home mother with a number of servants to take care of household chores, to a life with a demanding, full-time job and running a household with minimal help. In my case, I was trying to adjust to the change in status from being a senior faculty member at a college with all the attendant prestige and perks, to being a graduate student, almost at the bottom of the academic totem pole. Further, we had moved from a close-knit community of colleagues and friends living in a slow paced and very informal setting, to a life in an apartment with very little interaction among residents – and a great degree of formality associated with such interactions. Initially, it felt as if we had suddenly switched over from a leisurely and peaceful ride on a country road to a high-speed motorway – from a journey that gave us the time and opportunity to enjoy the activities and vistas surrounding us, to a hectic trip which we could survive only by staying alert, strictly following the formal rules of the road and avoiding any unplanned or unannounced actions. In spite of being fully aware of, and anticipating these differences, it took us some time to adjust to and feel comfortable in the Western environment.

An unexpected blessing

By the middle of our second winter in Ottawa, I had completed the requisite course requirements for my Ph.D. and was exploring suitable topics for my dissertation. Margaret had settled into her work as a visiting public health nurse and Ravi was generally happy at his new daycare. Although we still did not own a car, we were better prepared for the long and bitter Ottawa winter. Our spirits were higher and our pockets were fuller as we approached the Christmas and New Year holidays. We welcomed 1970 with greater hope and expecting to continue on the path to prosperity and success without encountering any major diversions. However, early in the year we discovered that in spite of using an IUD for contraception, Margaret had become pregnant and the baby was due in late June. We were planning to have a second child some time soon, although not exactly at this point, while I was in the middle of my Doctoral work and Margaret needed to work to sustain our modest lifestyle. Nevertheless, some higher power had already determined the time and place for the event and we were optimistic that we would be able to meet the upcoming challenges with some help and support from family and friends.

After breaking the news to family and friends, we decided to carry on as usual until the early spring. We assumed that as per Western tradition, the baby would be born in an Ottawa hospital and Margaret's mother would probably join us for a while to help when we brought the baby home. With the arrival of spring, we started planning for the changes that would be needed to accommodate the arrival and care of our new baby. To this end, we decided to sublet our current apartment and look for a less expensive place, as well as to get a used car that would alleviate our transportation problem – especially with a small baby during the cold Ottawa winters. While we were mulling over these and other practical matters, we were presented with an option which would resolve the dilemma we faced. Margaret's elder brother and his wife, who were now living on the family farm, proposed that both Margaret and Ravi live with them at the farm during the summer until after the baby was born, while I could take time off from my studies to visit them from time to time. We were obviously not in a position to decline such a kind and generous offer.

We breathed a great sigh of relief and started preparing in earnest for the upcoming changes in our living arrangements. Fortunately, we were able to sublet our apartment, along with the furniture, to an out-of-town visiting academic for the summer. I rented a small furnished room within walking distance of the University. It did not offer any cooking facilities and the owners of the house were a nice Chinese couple, which meant the house had a permanent and pervasive aroma of Chinese cooking. Since I planned to spend most of my waking hours at my office or the computer labs at the University; the room was essentially a sleeping pad. The room and my living arrangements were similar to those in Toronto during my last sojourn in Canada, but the circumstances were, of course, markedly different. I was also able to buy an inexpensive used car from a fellow student who was going back to his home in Africa – a Chrysler Valiant with a good engine, a rusting body and an automatic shift that required pressing buttons to shift gears. I was always afraid that I would press the wrong button while travelling at 100 km/h on a highway – maybe some people did exactly that because I never came across this feature ever again.

On the first day of May we handed over the apartment keys to the new tenants, said goodbye to our friends in the apartment complex, and made the four-hour drive to Margaret's family farm. It was my first time to venture on such a long car drive on a highway. I was nervous and tense, and avoided exceeding the speed limits or trying to pass another vehicle on the two-lane highway. I stayed on at the farm for a couple of days to visit with Margaret's family and see that Margaret and Ravi were comfortably settled. After heartily thanking Margaret's family for their generosity, I was on my way back to Ottawa for a summer of separation and loneliness. I was reminded of the character Tom Ewell plays in The Seven Year Itch, a film made famous by the scene of Marilyn Monroe's skirt flaring above a subway grate. Like him, I was going to be a summer bachelor, but I was certainly not expecting a Marilyn Monroe to drop in to keep me company. Except for driving down to Lindsay on alternate weekends, I spent most of my waking hours doing front-end work on my Doctoral research and preparing for the upcoming 'Comprehensive Examinations' – a dreaded milestone for Ph.D. candidates in most North American universities.

By the middle of June, I expected news from Margaret that the arrival of the baby was imminent. After one false start and a mad rush to Lindsay, in the early morning of the seventh day of the seventh month in the seventieth year of the century, I received the call from Margaret's sister-in-law that our daughter had finally made up her mind to make her *debut*. I drove down to the farm to spend the next couple of weeks with the family and to participate in the celebration of our daughter's arrival. During this time I tried my hand, for the first time, at the typical farming chores, such as cutting and bailing hay and cultivating fields and preparing them for the next crop. I enjoyed driving the old tractor, surrounded by the vistas of open Ontario farmland, dotted with distant farm houses. The sun and open air were exhilarating, although I did get sunburned for the first and only time in my life. My family in India owned a fair amount of farmland, as landlords, but we had never been farmers in the sense of being involved in the day-to-day operations. That was left to paid help or some type of sharecropping arrangement with local farmers. As well, the farming methods in India at that time were very primitive and mechanized farming was a rarity.

We were somewhat amused at the reversal of prevailing traditions around the births our two children. At our son's birth in India, according to Indian tradition, Margaret should have gone to her parents' home for the pre- and post-delivery period, rather than staying with me. On the other hand, when our daughter was born in Canada, Margaret went to her childhood home rather than staying with me in Ottawa until the baby arrived. We decided to name our daughter Malini Ruth: the first name after a character in a play by the Indian Nobel Laureate Rabindra Nath Tagore, and choosing Ruth for the middle name, which was the same as Margaret's middle name.

Recovery and return to Jabalpur

As planned, in early September we loaded up our car, thanked Margaret's family for their generous and extended hospitality and headed back to Ottawa. Margaret's mother was kind enough to accompany us to share some of the initial challenges of settling into a routine with a new baby. We decided to spend the night at a motel overlooking Silver Lake about 50 miles from Ottawa so that we could arrive in the early morning because we still had to move our furniture from the old apartment into the new one. A couple of our friends helped us with the move and by the evening we were ready to start this new phase of our life in Canada. We realized that we were still not fully out of the water, although we had survived the deepest and most worrisome part with the timely and generous help of Margaret's family. On the other hand, we could see with some hope and optimism, the distant shore, and a happy ending to the latest challenge of our life's journey.

Soon after we moved into our new home, we were faced with a problem that we had not given much thought to during the summer. It was the beginning of the school year and Ravi was now five years old and he needed to enrol in a public school to start his formal education. However, the nearest public school was just under a mile from our apartment building which meant that he was not eligible for a door-to-door ride in a school bus. It was a difficult decision to let a five-year-old child walk alone for such a distance through winding streets with no sidewalks. But Ravi took it all in his stride and did not seem to have any reservations or complaints. I usually gave him a ride to his school as often as I could on my way to the University – especially in the winter. In retrospect, we often wondered whether we were somehow negligent or not protective enough compared to current parenting standards.

Malini was a healthy and mostly happy baby and by the time she was around six months old she was essentially weaned from breastfeeding. At this point, Margaret started to take on a few evening assignments or night shift work as a 'private nurse', either at one of the hospitals or at private residences. Financially, we were again going through a rough patch, and any additional money was a welcome relief. Fortunately, in the spring a Senior Citizens' home opened just behind our apartment building. Margaret soon secured a position as an evening or night Duty Nurse for a few nights a week. It was a boon in terms of providing a more regular contribution to our family finances, and, after a while, helped us to put aside a modest nest egg for the proverbial rainy day. On a more personal level, taking our cue from the family planning billboards that had surrounded us in India, which depicted a young couple with two happy and healthy children and the headline *"WE TWO AND OUR TWO"*, we decided we had achieved an ideal family unit. To ensure that it would stay that way, we decided that the best solution was for me to undergo a vasectomy. It turned out to be a reasonably simple procedure performed in a physician's office and we have never regretted the decision.

We were so busy in our day-to-day life that the next two years went by very quickly. In spite of some anxious periods during those four years, we came out at the other end wiser and richer, both literally and figuratively. Both of us had enhanced our professional credentials – I by achieving the highest academic degree in my profession and Margaret by gaining additional professional experience in her field. We were also enriched by the addition of a healthy, happy and beautiful daughter to our family. To our surprise, we found that thanks to Margaret's steady contributions, at the end of these four years our bank balance was much better than we could have expected, given some of the hard times that we had faced in recent years.

By the end of September 1972, we were winding down our household in Ottawa and getting ready to pull stakes once again and move back to the opposite side of the world. Although we had never contemplated not returning to India after the completion of my Doctoral studies, we were doing so with mixed emotions. On one hand, we were leaving behind one part of our family and a score of good friends that we had made over the past four years, and on the other we were looking forward to reuniting with the other part of our family and joining the community of friends and colleagues that we had said goodbye to four years ago. This was the emotional price we incurred when we entered into a marriage that spanned two distant continents. On the last day of September, 1972, we said goodbye to Margaret's family and a few friends at the Dorval airport in Montreal and boarded a KLM flight en route to New Delhi via Amsterdam.

As the Boeing 707 aircraft flew east leaving the Montreal city lights behind, I thought about my last departure for India from the same airport almost eight years ago. At the time, I was single and contemplating the rather unorthodox step of making a Canadian girl from a WASP back ground my bride and partner for life. In spite of my initial misgivings about potential reactions and repercussions from my family and friends, things had played out much better than we could have ever imagined. This time around, we were going back as a happy and loving family with few concerns about our private life as a family in the global village. However, I was not sure that my long grind towards earning a Ph.D. would pay off, and that my professional life would turn out to be as fulfilling and rewarding as my family life.

INDIA (1972 – 1974)

****

CHAPTER 14

Back to academia and stirrings of discontent

We landed at the Delhi Airport in the early morning of October 2nd, 1972. We were jetlagged and exhausted after the long journey and looking forward to a hot shower and an extended rest. However, we were soon made aware that we were back in the land of the bureaucrats and any thoughts of speedy passage through the chaotic Indian Customs and Immigration system at the airport was just wishful thinking. It took us over two hours to convince the Customs Officer that all the items in our baggage came under the category of what is known as 'transfer of household' and they had been in use for at least six months and were exempt from customs duties. Most bureaucrats in India and perhaps in most countries around the world operate under the assumption that a person is 'guilty until proven otherwise' which places the burden of proof on the innocent person caught in their web. Finally, we were released from the web but not before the Customs Officer insinuated that he had done us a big favour and in return, we could help his son get admission at the Engineering College where I was employed.

On arriving at the hotel near Connaught Circus, the main business and shopping area in New Delhi, we had a quick breakfast and spent the rest of the morning and early afternoon getting some much needed rest. When we stepped out of the hotel in the late afternoon for a stroll through the shopping complex which is usually bustling with people, we found that the place was essentially deserted and everything was closed up because October 2nd happened to be Mahatma Gandhi's birthday, now also called International Non-violence Day, a national holiday in India. The night was not as quiet and restful as we would have wished because late at night Ravi developed such a nasty and incessant cough that we had to summon the hotel physician for medical assistance. Fortunately, he administered some medication that alleviated Ravi's stress and we were all able to get a few hours of sleep. The next morning we were again at the airport and boarded a tiny commuter plane for Bhopal, our State capital. Even though

I had provided sufficient advance notice of my imminent return to the relevant bureaucrats, this detour was necessary so that I could see them in person and prod them to complete the necessary paper work so that I could return to my teaching job in Jabalpur.

Setting up a household again

It took a couple of days before the required paperwork was completed and we could finally take the night train to Jabalpur. On our arrival the next morning we were met by a number of colleagues and friends. One of the professors in my department was kind enough to offer their guest room, until we could arrange accommodation of our own in the staff colony. Soon after assuming my position at the college, we took a few days off to make a short visit to my hometown to see my family who were anxious to see us – especially Malini, the new addition to our family. The ancestral home appeared unchanged, except for the fact that the house was now fitted with electric lighting (no more kerosene lamps). The operations of the household still revolved around my father's strict daily routine, with little variation from one day to the next. The contrast between the life we had left behind in the West only a week ago, and the life we were now experiencing could not have been more pronounced.

When we returned from our short trip, we were glad to learn that we had been temporarily assigned a small two bedroom house within the college residential campus until a house appropriate to my position in the academic hierarchy became available. Fortunately, Pandit, our former cook was still available and anxious to take over the responsibility of stocking and running the kitchen for our family. We enrolled Ravi in a school operated by Catholic nuns which was located about a mile from our residence. Pandit had to give him a ride on his bicycle in the morning and pick him up in the afternoon from the school. We also retained a private tutor so that Ravi could quickly learn to read, write and re-learn spoken Hindi, the local language – which was a compulsory subject in the school curriculum. Finally, in late December we learned that we would be able to move into a much larger bungalow at the beginning of the New Year.

We had a rather quiet Christmas, mainly because our living arrangements were still in flux awaiting long-term housing and the arrival of the rest of our household items from Canada. During this period we received notice that the packages sent by ship from Ottawa had arrived and were waiting for customs' clearance at the port authority in Bombay. Instead of hiring an intermediary to look after clearing the items through customs and shipping them to us, we decided to travel to Bombay and look after it ourselves, taking the opportunity to have a brief family vacation to celebrate the festive season. The vacation part was pleasant and fun for the children. However, the business part of the trip could not have been more ill-timed. When we arrived at the customs warehouse on the Bombay wharfs, the place looked like a madhouse. We soon realized that the chaos had resulted from a huge influx of displaced persons of Indian origin, who had been expelled from Uganda by the brutal regime of Idi Amin. The refugees had brought goods with them that they had accumulated over many generations, in order to set up residence once again in a land that their forefathers had sailed from centuries ago. On one hand, it was frustrating to navigate through this chaos, but on the other we could not help but empathize with these innocent people, who were victims of another mad dictator, like Hitler.

When we returned from Bombay with our packages from Canada, our new residence in the staff colony was ready for us to move in. Our unit was quite spacious and featured a large front yard, with a view of the distant lake and the hills beyond from the front veranda. The house included a large central room for use as a living/dining area which led into a kitchen/pantry and a large courtyard with banana and papaya trees at the back. The rest of the space was taken up by three bedrooms, two washrooms, a study and a guest bedroom. On one side of the house, there stood a huge mango tree whose thick branches extended over the courtyard providing much needed shade in the summer, as well an ample supply of raw fruit for making mango pickles. Beyond the walled courtyard at the back we had servant quarters. These were occupied by our cleaning lady, and her large family which included a blind son and a daughter who was Malini's age and also her frequent playmate. We were settling back nicely into the slow-paced life style that we had left behind four years ago with a few extra luxuries that we could now enjoy – including a small refrigerator and a new, compact car, although still no telephone. One of the great pleasures of owning the car was being able to drive in comfort to my hometown and not having to endure the tiring, tedious and time-consuming journey on the dilapidated and noisy inter-city buses. It was indeed a special occasion when my father agreed to take a ride in the car to visit a family friend in a nearby village – perhaps his first ride ever in a car and definitely his first excursion beyond our town boundaries in many decades.

A frustrating trip abroad

Before leaving Canada, I had submitted a paper based on my Ph.D. work to an upcoming international conference being held at the University of Delft in the Netherlands the following summer. Soon after the New Year I was notified by the Conference Paper Selection Committee that my paper had been accepted. I quickly discovered that if I wanted to attend the international conference in the Netherlands that summer, I would be facing intense hurdles. The college had no budgetary provisions for the staff to participate in academic conferences, either national or international. This meant that I had to spend a large amount of time and effort in chasing alternate sources of funding for the trip which involved constant battles with the entrenched bureaucracies. The frustration was further compounded by the lack of even basic telecommunications infrastructure in the country, which resulted in unnecessary travel and much wasted time. Without a telephone at our residence and no direct dialling for intercity calls, I remember sitting next to a telephone at a friend's house for almost five hours, waiting to get a long distance connection between Jabalpur and Delhi. It was not an uplifting experience.

After spending many, long frustrating hours in correspondence and personal visits to various agencies and individuals who could provide financial assistance for my trip, I managed to line up sufficient funds for my return air fare to the Netherlands a few weeks before the scheduled date for the conference. However, I still did not have a green light from my employers, nor did I have the necessary clearance from the federal authorities for travel to a foreign country which would involve an outlay of hard currency – a commodity that was perennially in short supply in India, in those days. By the time I received the green light from my employers, it was so close to the conference date that I had only a few hours to pack my bags and catch a train to Delhi where I spent the next two days visiting various federal ministries and the Reserve Bank of India to line up the final approval for the foreign trip. I finally boarded an Air India flight for Frankfurt en route to Amsterdam with ten US dollars in my wallet, which was the amount of foreign currency I was allowed to take out of the country. I greatly regretted having cashed all of my Canadian-Dollar travellers' cheques on my arrival in India, since they would have come in handy under the circumstances. However, I was expecting some Canadian funds to be transferred to me on my arrival in the Netherlands, which would cover the conference registration fee, as well as my living expenses while at the conference.

The bureaucratic nightmare that I had to go through to make the short trip happen, as well as the financial hardships that I had to endure while I was at the conference, left me feeling disillusioned and humiliated. I was greatly disappointed by the utter lack of support or sympathy at every level of the bureaucracy that seemed to have no interest in promoting academic excellence or encouraging those few who endeavoured to strive for it. Soon after the start of the monsoon season, the college academic year started in July and the campus was flooded with new and returning students, all hopefully anxious to get on with their studies. However, within a few months it became clear that in the last four years, the student population had become more politicized and the professional politicians were using students as tools to achieve their own goals in the wider political arena. The political landscape in the country had changed markedly during our absence and faith in the political process had declined among the population. By the start of the winter session things started to get ugly, with students frequently boycotting classes over issues that had little relevance to academic matters and were quite often prompted and encouraged by external political entities with their own axes to grind. It soon became apparent that the problem of ongoing student apathy to learning and upper management's disinterest in promoting academic excellence among the college staff were not going to be resolved in the foreseeable future. Under the circumstances, I could not envision wasting my professional education and experience by spending the rest of my career in such an unhealthy academic atmosphere.

Exploring career alternatives

The window of opportunity to salvage my professional career was narrowing rapidly mainly because I was already past my fortieth birthday and was afraid that I might soon become too complacent to take action. Since we were still committed to raising our family in India, I initially attempted to find a suitable position in a nationally recognized technical institution which would offer an opportunity for a more rewarding and satisfying professional career. In this quest, I was fortunate to find a position as a Professor of Communications Engineering at the University of Roorkee through a rather rigorous selection process and was told to expect a formal offer in the early summer, with a start date in July.

Roorkee is a town located near the foothills of the Himalayas about 175 kilometres north of New Delhi. It was a small village consisting of a few mud huts until in 1840 the British rulers of India (British East India Company) decided to undertake the major engineering project of building the Upper Ganges Canal to provide irrigation for the large tract of land between the Ganges and Yamuna rivers. Roorkee became a garrison town for the army engineers and the centre of operations for building the canal. Roorkee College was established to train local youth in civil engineering so that they could assist in the building of the canal. From these humble beginnings it developed into an Engineering University. Considering the long and distinguished history of the institution and its growing reputation as a centre for engineering education, I considered myself lucky to have secured a staff position there and started marking time until we could move to Roorkee at the end of the summer.

Around this time, we faced a rather frightening medical situation when we noticed a growing lump on Ravi's face. We needed to have it promptly diagnosed and treated because it could represent some form of malignant tumour. We first sought professional advice from the local medical community, ranging from a family physician to a professor of surgery at the local Medical College. These consultations convinced us that the local medical talent and facilities were not adequate to deal with the problem. We decided to take Ravi to the All India Institute of Medical Sciences (AIIMS) in New Delhi – one of the few hospitals in India at the time with highly trained staff and state-of-the-art facilities. After a long train journey filled with delays and anxiety we managed to reach New Delhi. The next morning we took Ravi to the AIIMS. After consultation with a surgeon, surgery to remove the tumour was scheduled for the next morning. After about four days, we learned that the pathologist's report was negative for malignancy and Ravi was discharged from the hospital. Margaret and I both felt an immense sense of relief and thanked the powers-that-be for the positive outcome. We went back to Jabalpur to face the heat and dust of another Indian summer. However, as it turned out, our sense of relief was premature, and our days of constant anxiety and uncertainty were to return soon.

CHAPTER 15

At the crossroads again, facing hard choices

The summer of 1974 was no different from past summers that we had lived through in India. The days were filled with punishing heat under cloudless skies making it unpleasant to go outside except in the early part of the morning or after the late afternoon. That year, the large mango tree next to our courtyard wall at the back was unusually fecund with its branches loaded with abundant fruit. The green mangoes were a great attraction for the neighbourhood urchins who threw stones and sticks at the branches in the hope of dislodging a few mangoes, which they would eat with relish in spite of the tartness of the raw fruit.

After the hectic trip to New Delhi for Ravi's surgery, the early part of summer was comparatively quiet except for occasional short visits from my relatives and a trip to my hometown for a family wedding. We were in a sort of holding pattern, anxiously awaiting the arrival of the formal job offer from Roorkee so that we could decide where our future home would be. Finally the formal offer arrived towards the end of May and at first glance it seemed to be well below my expectations. I was still optimistic and hoped that a mutually satisfactory compromise could be reached through further discussion and negotiation. In this spirit, I decided to make a personal trip to Roorkee to talk to the various players, although the journey was long and uncomfortable in the summer heat. However, after talking to the relevant people, including the Vice Chancellor of the University, I learnt that the University was not as autonomous as I had believed and that they were regretfully unable to modify the offer. Since the University had been established under the charter of the provincial government, which was also its major source of funding, it was not only bound by the bureaucratic rules and regulations of the government but was also subject to some degree of political influence in its operations.

A difficult decision

I was disappointed by the turn of events, although not as much by their reluctance to modify the job offer as by the underlying bureaucratic reasons for their reluctance. I started to doubt whether Roorkee would provide the working atmosphere that I had hoped for and was having second thoughts about taking this particular path in our life's journey. I was already trying to get away from the clutches of one large bureaucracy, which I had learned to live with, in my present job, and did not want to commit the folly of falling into the clutches of another, largely unfamiliar, bureaucratic web. I was hoping to find an organization, preferably in India, that provided a high degree of autonomy, encouraged individual job performance and believed in just and fair rewards based on merit alone. I had hung my hopes on this move to Roorkee to provide such a working environment, and did not have a Plan B, and so was caught in a major dilemma. When I sought advice from some of my more senior professional colleagues about my dilemma, it was their unanimous opinion that it would be difficult, if not impossible, for me to find an organization in India that would meet my criteria. Bureaucracy, politics and influence-peddling were now so pervasive in India that no university or institution was completely free from the effects of the national malaise. This assessment was disheartening, and it finally led me to think about pursuing professional fame and fortune outside of India. With my past professional and personal connections in Canada, the obvious choice was to return to Canada on a more permanent basis. I did not have much more time to get my professional future on the right path. I was now forty two years old and at the midway point of my professional life with only a narrow window of opportunity to salvage my moribund professional career.

Standing at the cross roads, I was torn between the two options. On an intellectual level I was pulled towards the road which promised recognition and rewards for my professional contributions, and on the emotional level the alternate choice ensured continuity with the life style I had intimately known, and offered comfort among my extended family, my community, my cultural roots, my homeland and my heritage. Ultimately, intellect won over emotion, and I reluctantly decided to become a full fledged immigrant to Canada. I knew that the decision would be pivotal, not only in shaping my professional career but also for the future of every member of our family. When I shared the idea with Margaret and sought her opinion, her response was that from her perspective she was perfectly happy living in India and loved being part of my extended family. Fulfilling my professional ambitions was an important factor for her overall happiness, and if moving back to Canada was my preferred option, she would be equally happy to set up residence back in Canada where she and our children would be closer to her extended family. It is hard to say if she would have continued to hold the same view five, ten, or fifteen years in the future, especially if our lack of financial resources prevented her from occasionally visiting her family in Canada and reconnecting with her roots – this had been my father's primary reservation about our intercontinental marriage. It was also difficult to imagine that ten or fifteen years in the future when our children would have grown up and left home, Margaret, an intelligent, articulate, and well educated, professional woman, would be satisfied in playing the role of a stay-at-home Indian housewife, drinking tea and exchanging gossip with the neighbourhood ladies.

Having agreed on this direction, and determined to embark on it as soon as it was practical to do so, the next immediate task was to break the news to my father and the rest of my family. My father was, of course, unhappy to see us move permanently so far away from home and family. His concern that we would be unable to visit him and the family often enough, was partly alleviated when I assured him that once we were properly settled in Canada, we would have sufficient means to visit regularly and if needed, we would be able to help them financially. By the time this decision was finalized and I had sent my regrets to Roorkee, it was already nearing the end of June and I needed to start exploring job prospects in Canada. To this end, I sent my résumé to some of my contacts in Ottawa, including one of my professors at Carleton University who was now the Dean of Engineering. He was kind enough to offer me a temporary assignment to teach a couple of graduate courses in the upcoming autumn session starting in September. I accepted the offer with the view that it would give me sufficient time to find a more permanent position, which generally required face-to-face interviews and evaluations. Once again we were caught in the process of moving house from one side of the world to another – a task made a lot more onerous due to the procedures involved in arranging foreign travel from India at the time. The next month was a whirlwind of activity – selling household items that we could not ship including the car, packing and shipping items to Canada, arranging for necessary travel documents, and travelling to visit family members to say goodbye.

One of these visits was to my uncle and his family with whom I had lived while completing my high school and early college education. They now lived in a town not far from the world famous temple complex of Khajuraho, which is a UNESCO world heritage site. The complex consists of 22 (out of an original 80) temples, which combine highly original temple architecture and sandstone sculptural frescos of surprising quality. The sandstone frescos surrounding the outside walls of the temples depict the everyday secular and spiritual life of the period, of which, according to ancient Hindu and *Tantric* traditions, sex is an important and integral part. About ten per cent of the frescos are devoted to explicit erotic scenes which are some times referred to as the *Kamasutra* in stone. *Kamasutra*, happens to be more than just an exclusive sex manual describing love making positions *à la* 'Joy of Sex'; it is a guide to virtuous and gracious living that discusses the nature of love, family life and other aspects of pleasure.

Our visit to Khajuraho and a picnic with my uncle and his family on a wayside stop was one of the most relaxing and memorable days before we departed from India. By the end of August, all of the preparations for our departure were in place and we made a brief visit to my ancestral home to say our final goodbye to my father and reassure him of my intention to visit him as often as possible. We left Jabalpur permanently on a rainy night in early September. It was a very touching scene with a large number of my students and colleagues who gathered at the railway station to bid us farewell. They had brought loads of marigold and rose garlands that filled our carriage. We spent a couple of days in Delhi picking up our plane tickets and doing some last minute shopping for gifts to take back to Canada. On September 7th, 1974 we boarded an Al Italia flight en route to Montreal via Rome with a mixture of trepidation and hope about what lay ahead around the abrupt turn we had made in our life's journey. This day was also Margaret's birthday and the cabin crew were kind enough to serve us Champagne and cake for the occasion. We drank to her long life and to the fulfilment of our hopes and desires in the days, months, and years ahead, as I embarked on my life in Canada as an immigrant.

CANADA (1974 – 1990)

****

CHAPTER 16

An immigrant has landed

In the early afternoon of September 8th, 1974, our Al Italia flight landed in Montreal where we were welcomed by Margaret's family who drove us to Ottawa. Margaret, Ravi and Malini continued on to Lindsay to spend a week or two visiting family and friends while I stayed in Ottawa with friends to start my teaching duties at the University and look for suitable accommodation for the family. We rented a three bedroom townhouse in a complex off Baseline Road – a residential area close to shops and schools, not far from where we had lived before leaving for India. Initially, our household consisted mostly of items donated or loaned by friends and family. Once Margaret and the children joined me, the first priority was to get Ravi enrolled in a suitable neighbourhood public school and the next one was to acquire a car. We were able to get Ravi enrolled in a school within walking distance which he seemed to like and where he quickly started making friends. We were less successful, however, with the car: we ended up with a 'rusty Ford' which looked fine when we bought it, but its body fell apart within a couple of years.

During the early months after our arrival, my major task was to find a more permanent position in an organization where I could achieve my long-term professional goals and aspirations. After a number of interviews, I decided to accept a position as member of the scientific staff at Bell Northern Research (BNR). At the time, BNR was the research and development arm of Bell Canada, the largest telephone operating company in Canada and Northern Electric (later renamed Nortel Networks), a Canadian telecommunications equipment manufacturer. While academic research work at universities usually had few strings attached, research projects at BNR were mostly aimed at new telecommunication products and services or their enhancements. So, the research scientists at BNR could clearly visualize the potential contributions of their labour in a tangible way. BNR was also an equal opportunity employer in terms of gender, ethnicity and nationality and it adhered to a strict policy of performance-based compensation. I formally started working at BNR in the first week of January, 1975 while continuing to teach at Carleton University on a part-time basis.

Although I was now officially an immigrant to Canada, I was by no means a typical Canadian immigrant who often lands here with a sketchy understanding of the country's culture, history and geography, with few friends or family to provide a soft landing. I had already gone through the initial phase of adjustment when I first came to Toronto in 1961. By now I had already spent almost six years as a student in Canada and had been married to a Canadian girl for almost a decade, and we had family and friends to help us settle quickly and make us feel at home. In the beginning, our finances were barely adequate to cover the rent, the purchase of a car and the daily living expenses of a family of four. To mitigate our short-term financial stress, Margaret found a position as a psychiatric nurse at the local children's hospital. The hospital was located quite far from our house and she had to work mostly the evening shift on weekends. This meant that she got off work almost at midnight. Margaret could not drive and using public transport to get home was impractical at that time of night. The only option was for me to pick her up at the end of her shift when the children were already in bed. Ravi at this point was just nine and a half years old and too young to officially babysit. In retrospect, I think I was taking a significant risk by leaving the children alone and driving through often nasty Ottawa winter nights, with the possibility of getting into an accident. Even now, when I think about it, I thank my stars that nothing untoward happened during those late night excursions.

Our friends Barbara and Bruce Baker, who were back in Ottawa after spending a year in the South of England, were now living in a townhouse in Kanata, a suburban community in the west end of Ottawa. The original community of Kanata was a mixed-dwelling community with small clusters of houses connected by open park spaces and walking and biking paths, where the dwellings blended in with the local terrain as much as possible. It was a self-sufficient community with good public schools, recreational facilities and other amenities. The Bakers were keen that we should move to Kanata which would be an excellent location for bringing up our children until they were ready to leave home for post secondary education. By early spring, with a few months working at BNR and a decent salary supplemented by Margaret's part time nursing we were starting to feel that the worst of our financial stress was easing off. When the townhouse next to the Bakers went on the market later in the spring, we decided to take the plunge and bought it with a minimum down payment and a relatively hefty mortgage. We moved into our first ever house which we (technically) owned, thereby taking the first step in a typical immigrant's journey by assuming a mortgage and starting to chase an immigrant's dream.

In the summer of 1975, we moved into our townhouse in Kanata and we were extremely happy with our decision. The best feature of the unit was that it backed on to extensive woodlands that residents could use for recreational purposes, such as cross- country skiing, horse back riding and growing vegetables in the summer. Our housing cluster was mainly populated by young professionals, most with young families, and there were ample opportunities for the adults and children to socialize and make friends. The children's schools were within a short, safe walking distance and the constant interest and involvement of the community members in their children's education and development made sure that the schools maintained a high standard. It was a bonus to have the Bakers as next-door neighbours, especially because I was a complete novice in the area of home maintenance and improvement, having never used a carpentry tool until then. Bruce helped me launch into the world of DIY (Do It Yourself), an essential requirement for a house owner in Canada, where labour rates are prohibitively high compared to India where labour is cheap and in ample supply. Soon with Bruce's guidance, I was finishing our basement to add additional living space which not only required extensive carpentry but also electrical wiring and lighting, flooring and a few other skills that I had not heard of. With this project under my belt, I now had enough confidence to tackle most day-to-day maintenance jobs in the house.

Not long after the end of 1975, we again faced a period of acute anxiety and concern. The growth on Ravi's cheek, which we thought had been successfully dealt with not long ago in India, had reappeared. This meant that the surgery in India had failed to completely capture the malignancy and the pathology report immediately following the surgery was inaccurate. Fortunately, two factors were working in our favour now. First, we were now part of the Canadian health care system which was not only world class but which also ensured universal coverage at no cost. Second, Margaret having been trained as a nurse and having worked in the Canadian health care system was well equipped to navigate through the system to ensure that Ravi was cared for by the best qualified physicians and treated at the best equipped hospitals. After two surgeries and aggressive radiation treatment at the Toronto Sick Children's Hospital, Ravi was discharged with a clean bill of health at the end of the summer of 1976, with bi-annual check ups scheduled at the Toronto Sick Children's Hospital for the next five years.

Needless to say, it was a great relief to learn that Ravi had come through this ordeal with no long-term harm except for a minor asymmetry on one side of his face resulting from the deep surgical incision to remove the diseased parotid glands. However, every time the date for his follow up visits approached, we would enter a phase of increasing anxiety until the results of the tests came out in our favour. Ravi ultimately grew up as a healthy and physically active individual and has regularly participated in marathons and triathlons. Following this difficult period, I started to wonder if the second-hand smoke from my smoking habit had contributed to his health problems and could adversely influence the future health of our children. After twenty years of smoking, initially cigarettes and later a pipe, one day in 1977 I stopped smoking, threw away my collection of pipes and have never smoked since.

CHAPTER 17

Chasing an immigrant's dream

By the autumn of 1977, I was feeling quite comfortable with my professional activities. The work at BNR was challenging and interesting, and the part-time teaching at the University kept me in touch with academia. I was encouraged to write and present a research paper based on my research at BNR at a prestigious conference in the United States. This experience with the process of preparing for and participating in the conference was completely different and effortless compared to my experience of trying to attend a scientific conference in Netherlands four years ago, when I was still in India and had to wrestle multiple layers of bureaucracy. Margaret was also becoming more involved in her own professional activities and was establishing useful contacts among local professionals in her field. Financially, we were starting to feel more secure and we thought that I should take some time off to visit with family and friends in India. Thereafter, I tried to visit my family in India every two years until my father passed away in 1983. I could not attend his funeral mainly because, in the absence of air-conditioning and refrigeration facilities, it is a common practice in India for funerals to take place within twenty-four hours after death.

However, I went home the next year to attend the rituals associated with the first anniversary of my father's death. My favourite uncle and his family had now moved into our ancestral home after he retired and he was now the nominal head and anchor of our extended family. The timing of my visit was unfortunate because while I was in my hometown, Indira Gandhi, the prime minister of India was assassinated by one of her Sikh bodyguards, ostensibly in retaliation for her decision to send in the army into the Golden Temple at Amritsar (holiest temple of Sikhism) to evict Sikh terrorists who were holed up there. Many of the armed terrorists occupying the temple were killed and part of the temple was damaged during the operation. The assassination was followed by widespread riots in which scores of Sikhs were killed and most of the country was locked down by strict curfews with all transportation systems shut down. The worst horrors of the riots made the international headlines and I was certain that Margaret and her family in Canada were watching the news, and worrying about my safety – especially because of my long and ample facial hair, which feature is universally associated with men of the Sikh faith.

In the meantime, I was stranded in my hometown with no means of communicating with Margaret because the town had no telephone service for international calling. Fortunately, after some time, the riots calmed down and bus and rail transport gradually improved. After travelling by a circuitous route and using multiple means of transport, I finally arrived safely in Delhi to catch my flight back to Canada. Margaret and our children met me at the Montreal Airport and were betting that I would walk out of the arrival gate *sans* facial hair. I was glad to be back in Canada and hoped that these unpleasant and unfortunate events were behind us. The use of military force to drive the terrorists out of the Golden Temple was a tactical mistake which not only cost the life of Indira Gandhi, as well as the lives of thousands of innocent Sikhs, but it also alienated the larger Sikh community in India and abroad. The repercussions were felt as far as Canada, when in June 1985 an Air India flight from Toronto was brought down near Ireland by a bomb placed by Sikh terrorists based in Canada, killing over three hundred Canadian citizens, mostly of Indian origin. The culprits who perpetrated the worst terrorist incident in Canadian history have never been convicted or punished for this heinous act, leaving the near and dear of the victims bewildered, frustrated and angry, and the rest of the population losing a great deal of faith in the competence of the law enforcement and justice systems in the country.

By the early 1980s, we were well on our way to achieving an immigrant's dream Both Margaret and I had full-time jobs which were professionally satisfying and financially rewarding. Both Ravi and Malini were doing well in school and were academically well positioned to enter universities of their choice after completing high school. I had been promoted to a position where I was managing a small team of scientists and engineers and was invited to represent my company and Canada at the International Telecommunication Union (ITU), a specialized agency of the United Nations (UN), headquartered in Geneva. Between the meetings of the ITU and participation in various national and international conferences to present technical papers, my international travels and contacts within the worldwide scientific community in my field were rapidly growing. For our 25th wedding anniversary in 1989, after short stays in Cologne and Paris for my ITU meetings, we went to a small village in the Swiss

Alps near Geneva where we spent the holidays hiking in the mountains and experiencing the cuisines of various restaurants in the area recommended by *Gourmet* magazine. We also upgraded to a larger single-family home in the same Kanata neighbourhood – a bungalow with four bedrooms, three bathrooms, a two-car garage and a swimming pool.

Ravi was heavily into science and mathematics in his high school years and acquired one of the initial models of the Personal Computers developed by Apple. He used it to develop a science project called "A Computer Assisted Tour of Einstein's Theory of Relativity". The science project won him various awards including the first prize in the Canada-wide Science Fair for high school students. Ravi also excelled in national and international mathematics competitions and was a summer intern at BNR during his senior high school years. It was clear that his future was in the field of mathematics and computer science, so he enrolled at the University of Waterloo. However, one day in early spring while I was attending an ITU meeting in Madrid, I received a frantic telephone call from Margaret who said that Ravi was not very happy at Waterloo and he wanted to go to Japan and learn more about their next-generation computer project. With our half-hearted blessings he soon travelled to Tokyo where, for almost a year he supported himself by teaching English to Japanese children and occasionally posing for some risqué Japanese magazines.

Finally, Ravi returned to Canada, spending a few summers working at Xerox's Palo Alto Research Centre (Xerox PARC). He also spent a year or more trying to become a modern dancer but ultimately decided that pursuing a dancing career on a full-time basis was not his cup of tea. He then enrolled at the University of Toronto and quickly graduated with a degree in mathematics and was back working in the field of computer science in Silicon Valley in California. After various jobs in Silicon Valley, it was no surprise that Microsoft was glad to acquire his talents. It seems somewhat befitting that as a cancer survivor, his current research project at Microsoft is in the area of 'genome sequencing' which, in the not too distant future, could enable highly customized treatments for individual cancer patients and has the potential of greatly increasing survival rates from this insidious disease, often labelled as: 'The Emperor of all Maladies"

Malini, our daughter, turned out to be equally intelligent and creative, although she did not focus her energy and attention on a specific area during her school years. She had an altogether different personality and from an early age showed a penchant for making friends and maintaining these friendships over long periods. However, she was recognized as a Canada Scholar and was consistently on the 'Dean's List', while pursuing a degree in Industrial Engineering at the University of Toronto After graduation; she followed her mother's footsteps and spent a year backpacking around Europe with one of her close friends. After working in Canada for a while, she moved to a city near Paris where her boyfriend (later to be her husband) and also an Industrial Engineer, was studying towards a MBA at the European Business School (INSEAD). After spending another year or so in Amsterdam they decided to return and settle in Toronto. By this time they were married and were seriously thinking of starting a family. They live in a late nineteenth century clapboard house in mid-town Toronto in a very friendly neighbourhood with a park and a good public school for their two sons right across the street from their house.

AUSTRALIA (1990 – 1992)

****

CHAPTER 18

A short and pleasant diversion

In the fall of 1989, just before we went to Switzerland for our 25th wedding anniversary, I attended a conference in Adelaide, South Australia that had been organized by the Teletraffic Research Centre at the University of Adelaide. I liked the University of Adelaide campus as well as the city of Adelaide, with its planned city centre and the surrounding hills and vineyards interspersed with clusters of gum trees. In the spring of 1990, I received an invitation from the Chairman of the Governing Body of the Research Centre at Adelaide to consider an 18-month assignment as its Director because the current Director had been called back to her permanent job in the United States The prospect of this new experience was very enticing on a professional as well as a personal level, and both Margaret and I were keen to avail ourselves of the opportunity, provided we could successfully overcome the potential obstacles. By this time, Malini was in her second year at the University in Toronto and Ravi was in a steady job in the Silicon Valley so we were 'empty nesters' with the freedom to spend some time 'down under'.

Fortunately by the middle of August the potential obstacles that we faced were resolved to our satisfaction – specifically, my employers were exceptionally generous and supportive in smoothing the way for our temporary stay in Australia. In early September, we handed over our keys to the tenants who were renting the house for the duration of our absence, and prepared to leave for Australia - a country whose geography and culture I had only imagined while reading A Town Like Alice by Nevil Shute a long time ago in India, and later from books by such well known Australian authors as Morris West and Colleen McCullough.

Following two weeks of hectic activity before our departure, we not only needed some R&R but also a little time to adjust our mindsets to the new experiences that lay ahead for us in Australia. To this end, we decided to spend a few days in Hawaii on our way to Adelaide. Ravi and Linda (his American girl friend later to be his wife) flew down to join us in Honolulu and make it a short family get together as well. We were booked in a hotel which was close to the famous Waikiki beach but not overlooking the beach itself. The morning after our arrival we walked down to Waikiki beach. We stood there admiring the blue waters of the Pacific Ocean with early surfers already riding the waves and the Diamond Head rising on our left. Behind us we could see the spacious hotel bar under a huge Banyan tree. For a few minutes, I just stood there with a feeling of *déjà vu* because the sights looked so familiar from movies such as From Here To Eternity and the long running TV series Hawaii Five-0 – so much so that I could almost hear Steve McGarrett the main character, tell his sidekick to 'Book 'em Danno' as he did at the end of most episodes. We spent the next few days either at the beach or visiting various sightseeing landmarks on the island. Finally on a Friday night we said goodbye to Ravi and Linda and boarded a flight to Sydney en route to Adelaide.

As the sun rose in the sky on Saturday morning our plane made its approach towards the Sydney International Airport. On the left of the plane we could see the two iconic landmarks of Sydney – the beautiful Sydney Opera House with its overlapping white shells capturing the morning sun, and the massive iron structure of the Sydney Harbour Bridge often referred as the 'coat hanger' by the locals because of its shape. After a short flight we arrived at the modest Adelaide Airport where we were met by Ronny Potter whom I was to replace as the Director. Ronny was an Australian who had been educated at the University of Adelaide, and had settled in the United States. She owned a townhouse in North Adelaide not far from the university. Fortunately, Ronny had agreed to rent us her fully furnished home and her car, for the period of our stay, which allowed us to get anchored and established in our new surroundings rather quickly and with minimum amount of stress. The house was in a very nice neighbourhood on a wide tree-lined street with a number of parks in the vicinity as well as well as a stone's throw from Melbourne Street, locally well known for its upscale boutique stores, restaurants and food and wine shops.

The next morning which was a Sunday, Ronny and a couple of colleagues from the University took us for a tour of the wineries around Adelaide. This wine and food tasting tour gave us the opportunity to spend the day going from one winery to another, sampling their wines and food prepared by their chefs. The following morning Ronny took us to the University and introduced me to the staff at the Research Centre as well as to the senior administrative staff of the University. Following a farewell lunch for her, she said her goodbyes and wished me a professionally fulfilling and personally enjoyable time in Adelaide. It did not take me long to settle into my new position because the job was not significantly different from my responsibilities in Canada i.e., supervising a number of scientists and engineers working on projects funded by the national and international telecommunication service providers in Australia. I already knew a number of key players in these Australian organizations through various international conferences and my activities with ITU/UN. The essential difference was that for all practical purposes, except for providing biannual financial and progress reports to the Management Board of the Research Centre, I was my own boss.

In the meantime, Margaret was enjoying her freedom from the nine-to-five routine and especially being away from her daily uncomfortable bus travels during the harsh Ottawa winters. Since she was ostensibly on 'study leave' from her employers in Canada, she started exploring the possibilities of attending some suitable courses at the University, and also started spending a few hours a week as a volunteer at the local UNICEF outlet both of which allowed her to make friends in the local community. We were also looking forward to the Christmas when Malini, our daughter was planning to join us for the holidays. As in Canada, when the Christmas season approached, the local shopping areas brought out their decorations and intensified their advertising for Christmas gift shopping. However, when the sun blazed so relentlessly every day and temperatures hovered near 40 degrees Celsius, all this festivity seemed rather out of place and it was hard for us to reconcile it with our memories of Canadian Christmases in a landscape covered with snow and freezing temperatures to match. We were happy living in Australia and felt at home with its people, politics, and culture. Aside from the differences in climate, geography and fauna and flora, we observed that Australians in general were more attached to British traditions and customs compared to Canadians. For example, we soon learned that an invitation for 'tea' actually means an invitation for dinner, and noticed that such traditional British fare as 'Devonshire Tea' (tea served with scones with clotted cream and preserves) and Cornish Pasties were common items in many restaurants and bakeries.

We were delighted when Malini flew in from Toronto to spend Christmas with us in Australia. Fortunately, we had been invited by one of Margaret's local friends from the UNICEF Outlet, for Christmas dinner at her house. They had a nice house in the Adelaide Hills with a spectacular view of the city from their living room. They had bought the house at an auction which seems to be a common way of selling and buying real estate in Australia. They had prepared a traditional Christmas dinner of roast turkey and hot Christmas pudding served in an elegant, festive setting. Before and after dinner we spent most of our time in or near the outdoor pool where it felt as if we were back in India in the middle of an Indian summer. As part of our holiday, before Malini travelled back to Toronto, we spent a few days at a nice little hotel on Kangaroo Island, a short boat ride from the nearby launching point of Port Jervis. The island is sparsely populated, but is a tourist attraction because of its beautiful sandy beaches which stretch for miles with hardly anyone in sight. It is also famous for its large population of marine animals, such as sea lions and walruses, who gather on the beaches around the island. While driving past a farmhouse on the island one afternoon, we noticed a sign offering 'Devonshire Tea'. We decided to stop and the lady of the house served us an excellent repast, including a nice chat about the history of the settlers on the island, on the large veranda of the tin-roofed farm house.

I was enjoying my work at the Research Centre and making friends in the University faculty. Under the terms of my appointment, I was also involved in a great deal of international travel to participate in the ITU meetings on behalf of my Canadian employers. The majority, although not all of these meetings took place at the ITU Headquarters in Geneva and each of them lasted from one to three weeks. With these frequent long stays in Geneva, the city on the lake had almost become my home away from home and I frequently stayed in the same room at the top floor of a small hotel on a short street off rue Lausanne. The large room came with a decent kitchen, bath and a good size terrace from which, on a clear day one could get a distant view of Mont Blanc on the other side of Lake Geneva. The location was convenient in that it was within walking distance of the UN complex, the quay Mont Blanc, the promenade along the lake, and the old town, with its many excellent restaurants and historical landmarks. The meetings outside Geneva were scattered around the globe and the locations were determined by the desire of a country to host a specific meeting.

Since my international travels kept me away from the office so frequently, our travels and explorations within Australia were limited to brief visits to Sydney and Melbourne and short holidays at nearby estate wineries. However, the next Christmas, we took a family holiday to spend a week in Hilo (on the big island in Hawaii) with Malini, Ravi and Linda. It was nice to spend some time with our children and enjoy the sights and sounds of a tropical island. It was an experience to see the effects of frequent volcanic activity on the island where the beaches were covered with black sand and many of the roads were blocked by the hardened lava flows across them. Our vacation ended on the New Year's Eve and we boarded our late evening flights back to our respective destinations. Because of the 'date line' Malini and Ravi arrived back in North America in plenty of time to participate in New Year Eve parties. We, on the other hand, welcomed the New Year on board the QANTAS flight to Melbourne with champagne flowing freely all through the night.

When we returned from our holidays in Hawaii, we realized that the end of my assignment at the University of Adelaide was fast approaching and in a few more months we would be packing to return home to Canada. Although I had been approached with an offer to establish and run another Research Centre at the University, we felt it would be unwise to make a career change at this stage in our lives – especially if it required us to be so far away from our children, family and friends back in North America. Although we felt very comfortable living in Australia, we felt rather removed and isolated from the main centres of important world events. Thus, it was with mixed emotions, that we bid goodbye to our Australian friends and colleagues who had made our time in Australia personally enjoyable and professionally enriching. We arrived back in Ottawa in the middle of March in 1992 to a city which was still in the grip of winter, with the sidewalks full of dirty snow and bone-chilling winds coming off the frozen Ottawa River. However, it did not take us long to settle down in the jobs that we had left behind, and relearn the ways of surviving the long Ottawa winter, drawing comfort from the fact that spring was just around the corner.

CANADA (1992 – 2012)

****

Chapter 19

Into the sunset years

The next decade of our personal and professional lives brought more highs than lows en route to becoming 'senior citizens' and to a life of relative solitude and reflection. I formally retired from my company in 1997, and Margaret did the same a few years later. However, I was retained as a consultant so that I could continue to represent the company and Canada at the ITU where I was then chairing a group of international experts responsible for developing standards for the next generation of mobile communication systems. This work at the ITU ultimately contributed to the explosive growth in cellular phones worldwide that we see today, not only in terms of their ubiquitous usage but also in the astonishing range of functionality of these portable wireless devices. This was a period of frequent international travel for me as well as for Margaret because she frequently accompanied me on my overseas and North American trips to attend ITU related meetings or scientific conferences.

After the end of my consulting contract in the year 2000, I was often invited by the Development Sector of the ITU to provide expert advice to developing countries on matters related to mobile communications. The last of these UN assignments took me back to Jabalpur in India where I was born and where I had started my professional career as a teacher at the local Engineering College and which I had reluctantly abandoned to immigrate to Canada almost thirty years ago. The three-month assignment was to develop a course on a wireless related application for the Telecommunication Training Centre which provided training facilities for scientists and engineers from across the country who were employed by India's National Telecommunications Authority. This final assignment as a UN Expert was a watershed moment and a highly symbolic event for me on a number of levels. It represented a high point on which to conclude my professional career and evoked the feeling of the local boy being honoured in his own locality. Most of all, along with the technical papers and books that I had published while working in Canada, this assignment provided a vindication for the difficult and life-changing decision which I made a long time ago to abandon my roots and seek professional fulfillment half a world away.

The trajectory of our personal and family life had moved along a more or less predictable path, one that was similar to most middle-class Canadian families. Both Ravi and Malini were now away from home and were getting established in their professional and personal lives. After a long courtship, Ravi and Linda got married in 1994 and they established their home in Seattle. Malini also got married in the year 2000 and she and Mike spent a few more years in Europe before returning to Canada and settling in Toronto where Malini completed her Master's degree. By the end of the millennium, we found that the marriages of many of our close friends in Ottawa had broken up and some of them had new partners and others had moved away. With time and circumstance, the close interactions and camaraderie we had enjoyed in past years with these friends and their families sadly decreased, thus gradually shrinking our social circle in Ottawa. In our advancing years we realized that for our psychological and physical sustenance we had to depend on each other and on our own family.

The year we came back from Australia, we decided that it was high time that we visited our family and friends in India. I had not been back since the first anniversary of my father's death in 1984 and Margaret had not returned after we left for Canada in 1974. We celebrated *Diwali* in my ancestral home bringing back pleasant memories of our first visit together for *Diwali* immediately after our marriage and honeymoon. We went back to India for family visits a number of times after that visit together in 1992 and greatly enjoyed the easy and spontaneous hospitality from family and friends. Unfortunately, the visits had to be discontinued when I developed some health problems that made such long and stressful trips impractical. Further, after my uncle who lived in our ancestral home after my father's death also passed away and sadly my ancestral home where I grew up was no longer inhabited by the Pandya family. Four of my siblings have also passed away and the remaining two are in their twilight years with accompanying health issues. Margaret is in a similar situation with respect to her family in Canada and our visits to Lindsay and her family farm are now few and far between. This being the natural order of things, we had no option but to reconcile with our gradually diminishing numbers of elders and peers in our respective families, while we looked back and acknowledged the love and support they provided when we most needed it.

Our last visit to India in early 2002 coincided with my last assignment for the UN in India. After that visit, we realized that in our advancing years, with the potential health problems that were hovering on the horizon, it would be beneficial if we lived closer to at least one of our children. The obvious choice was to pull up stakes in Ottawa where we were feeling increasingly isolated, and to establish our home in Toronto not only to be close to Malini and her growing family, but also because both of us had lived in Toronto in our younger years and Toronto was more easily accessible from most cities in North America and overseas. We moved to Toronto in 2003, and were lucky to find a condominium apartment in midtown in an architecturally and aesthetically attractive building. Malini and her family moved into a house close by so that we could see them almost every day during our morning and evening walks through the park in front of their house. After living there for seven years, although our two-storey condominium was very spacious and convenient, we found that the associated maintenance requirements were becoming rather stressful and expensive. In 2010, we sold the condominium apartment and moved into a very desirable and reputable rental property close to the University campus, with excellent services and easy indoor access to a large variety of stores, restaurants, entertainment facilities and public transport.

After a period of almost half a century, we had come full circle by returning to our old stomping grounds around the University of Toronto campus. Many of the landmarks that we explored during our courtship are still around, albeit with significant changes to their appearance and character. Yorkville, where we frequented the coffee houses and listened to contemporary folk singers, still attracts locals and tourists, but the coffee houses have now been replaced by upscale restaurants, bars, and boutiques as well as by a few condominiums with multi-million dollar price tags. Landmarks such as Holt Renfrew and Stollery's clothing store are still on Bloor Street, but the street now boasts wide sidewalks, lined with flower beds and trees and has become the home of prestigious retailers like Cartier, Tiffany, Gucci, Louis Vuitton and many more internationally known brands. Philosophers' Walk still connects Bloor Street to Hoskins Avenue near Trinity College, but it has lost its reputation of being the place that gay men would frequent for furtive encounters with partners – now it is not uncommon to see gay couples openly strolling hand in hand along Bloor Street. The influx of immigrants from around the world has completely changed the cultural and social mosaic of the city. It has now become one of the most cosmopolitan and ethnically diverse cities in the world and has forever lost its moniker of 'Toronto the Good'. Most of the residents of the largest city in Canada seem to feel comfortable in their skin, safe and secure in and out of their homes, and confident of their future in this country founded on the principles of 'peace, order and good government'.

As an immigrant here, I have certainly been enriched both materially and professionally for which I am eternally thankful. However, I also fervently hope that I have been able to contribute at least a few drops to the vast sea of cultural, social and technological progress that has and is taking place in this country and around the world, and that my difficult decision to migrate across the globe has not been in vain.

EPILOGUE

After a rainy night which has washed away the usual city smog, it is a bright sunny summer morning in Toronto. We have recently returned from Niagara-on-the-Lake where we celebrated my eightieth birthday with the family. In the best Indian tradition I am having my early morning cup of tea looking over the city from our twentieth floor apartment. In the distance I can see Lake Ontario with its surface shimmering in the morning sun, as well as the CN Tower, the iconic landmark of the city of Toronto, rising majestically in the sky. The rest of the cityscape is a forest of skyscrapers mostly condominium apartments with a scattering of tall cranes sticking over them like giraffes with their necks rising above the enclosures in a zoo. We are coming towards the end of our journey together which we started half a century ago in this very same city and the same neighbourhood – although the city and the neighbourhood have changed a lot and so have we. At our stage in life, our future is more or less predictable and of course, our past is behind us and cannot be altered. However, this does not keep us from occasionally thinking about the question raised in the famous Robert Frost poem *the road not taken*. At these times we look back on the critical forks that we encountered during our journey and consider where we would be now if we had chosen one of the other available roads.

Obviously, there were many random incidents, as well as a few conscious decisions that we made when faced with alternate choices which ultimately shaped the trajectory of our lives. Needless to say, the two most important decisions that I had to make were: to step away from my cultural heritage, with thousands of years of history and tradition behind it, to choose a bride from a different culture, different ethnicity and a different continent and to make her a part of my very tradition-bound extended family. The second decision which I made with great reluctance was to give up on the years I had invested in my academic and professional career in India and immigrate to a far away country in the hope of a more fulfilling professional life thus causing great deal of distress and disappointment to my family and friends in India. Except for some generalities, it is very difficult to imagine how each of our lives would have played out in the absence of these critical decisions. I can say with certainty though, that the road we decided to travel bestowed on us many personal, professional and economic benefits that may not have accrued otherwise.

On all counts, I believe Canada has treated me well and Canada's founding principles of peace, order and good government, supplemented by its very progressive Charter of Rights and Freedoms, gives me a sense of security and comfort as a proud citizen of the country. I have developed a great deal of affinity and attraction towards my adopted country, and I have few lingering doubts or regrets for taking the road that we took, which was sometimes challenging but never dull. The journey over the road which we ultimately travelled together nurtured and strengthened our love and respect for each other and enriched our lives in every possible way.

Nevertheless, memories of my life in India resurface from time to time – especially when I happen to watch a movie like Monsoon Wedding or read books like A Suitable Boy. However, I have no desire to go back because I realize that the places and people who shaped me from my childhood through adulthood and beyond exist only in my imagination, and in reality they have either changed beyond recognition or have disappeared from the landscape altogether. As Thomas Wolfe so aptly posits in the title of his novel: *You Can't Go Home Again.*

Where the mind is without fear and the head is held high;
Where knowledge is free;
Where the world has not been broken up into
fragments by narrow domestic walls;
Where words come out from the depth of truth;
Where tireless striving stretches its arms towards perfection;
Where the clear stream of reason has not lost its way
into the dreary desert sand of dead habit;
Where the mind is lead forward by thee into ever-
widening thought and action:--
Into that heaven of freedom, my Father let my country awake.
Rabindra Nath Tagore (1861 – 1941)
Nobel Laureate, poet, play write, philosopher and much more

Acknowledgements

Are owed to my wife Margaret for her review and comments on the innumerable drafts and for her unfailing conviction that the story was worth telling and that the way it was being told was worth listening to which was a critical factor in bringing this project to fruition. To our daughter Malini who provided many comments and corrections to the initial drafts, and to Barbara Baker our long-time friend and consultant on all matters concerning English language and literature, not only for her extensive editorial comments and corrections but also for her constant encouragement all through the long gestation period of the manuscript. Finally, it would be remiss on my part if I failed to acknowledge the immense contributions of our families and our friends on both sides of the globe who displayed an unprecedented spirit of generosity and inclusiveness and who were always ready to extend their helping hands whenever we encountered unexpected bumps along our journey

Thank you. Thank you. Thank you.